The
Compleat Clammer

Christopher R. Reaske

Illustrated By Suzanne T. Reaske

NICK LYONS BOOKS

For Mary K., my life-long friend

Copyright © 1986 by Christopher R. Reaske

All rights reserved. No portions of this book may be reproduced (except in the case of brief excerpts in reviews) without permission in writing from the publisher. Inquiries should be addressed to Nick Lyons Books, 31 West 21 Street, New York, NY 10010.

Library of Congress Cataloging-in-Publication Data

Reaske, Christopher Russell.
    The compleat clammer.

    Includes index.
    1. Clamming. 2. Shellfish gathering. 3. Cookery
(Clams) 4. Cookery (Shellfish) I. Title.
SH400.5.C53R43   1986   639'.44   86–2761
ISBN 0–941130–15–0
ISBN 0–941130–11–8 (pbk.)

Printed in the United States of America

10 9 8 7 6 5 4 3 2 1

Contents

Preface

This may be the first book written completely during high tide. More than once I have dashed off with my clam rake and abandoned my manuscript just as an idea was beginning to come clear. Alternating clamming with writing about clamming, thereby making, as Isaak Walton wrote of fishing in his *The Compleat Angler*, "a *recreation* of a *recreation*," has had its advantages. For me, clamming is enriched by a heightened awareness of the details of the environment. My ability to talk about clamming is directly related to my regular immersion in the settings of the shorelines I know and love best. Thus I would like to believe that what might be lost in continuity of thought has been compensated for by the shallowness of my research, so much of which was necessarily carried out at low tide.

The mysteries of the ocean and the seemingly bizarre behavior of its many inhabitants have always fascinated man. Countless writers, from Aristotle and Homer to Herman Melville and Rachael Carson, have confronted the ocean with their very being. To me, the activity of clamming is intensified by my ongoing education about clams, about how they live, move, and eat, and about the rich places they hold in history, literature, science, and the arts.

There is no easy way to express how much I have benefited, in writing *The Compleat Clammer,* from the work carried out in a variety of disciplines ranging from archeology to gastronomy. I have consulted virtually all the standard encyclopedias, dictionaries, lexicons, gazetteers, and general reference works. I have read relevant sections of more specialized reference works such as Norman Meinkoth's *The Audubon Society Field Guide to North American Seashore Creatures,* E. A. Martin's *Dictionary of Life Sciences,* Spector's *Handbook of Biological Data,* Grizimek's *Animal Life Encyclopedia,* G. E. MacGinitie and N. MacGinitie's *Natural History of Marine Animals,* countless articles published by different state departments of natural resources and marine research laboratories, articles in both popular marine journals, including many back issues of *Sea Frontiers* and more recent issues of *International Wildlife, National Geographic, Underwater Naturalist,* and a variety of more technical and scientific journals in ecology and marine biology, including *The Journal of Experimental Marine Biology and Ecology* and *Marine Biology.* I have benefited at Yale from the Kline Biology Library and the Library of the Yale School of Forestry and Environmental Studies, where the director of the library, Joseph Miller, assisted me with his computerized bibliographic retrieval system, secured some of the data for the Appendix, and led me to the *Oceanic Index* and other research tools.

There are numerous books cited during the course of the text, and all of them provided me with many evenings of good reading. Special thanks should be given here to several that were particularly helpful, including Willard Bascom's *Waves and Beaches,* Augusta Foote Arnold's *The Sea-Beach at Ebb Tide,* Euell Gibbons's *Stalking the Blue-Eyed Scallop,* John Hay and Peter Farb's *The Atlantic Shore,* Kenneth Gossner's *A Field Guide to the Atlantic Seashore,* William Cromie's *The Living World of the Sea,* Yvonne Tarr's *The Great East Coast Seafood Book,* Dorothy Sterling's *The Outer Lands,* James Dugan's *Man under the Sea,* R. Buchsbaum and L. J. Milne's *The Lower Animal: Living Invertebrates of the World,* Thor Heyerdahl's *American Indians in the Pacific,* G. H.

Luquet's *The Art and Religion of Fossil Man,* H. Obermaier's *Fossil Man in Spain,* and Carleton Coon's *The Hunting Peoples.* Whether interested in the clam's role in the evolution of man and in paleoecology, or in how mussels are served on certain coasts of France, all these writers, and many others, have deepened and enhanced my appreciation of clams and related shellfish.

Individuals have also helped me. My father, Herbert E. Reaske, has not only tracked down but discovered a number of interesting references to clams in such areas as literature, mythology, and the decorative arts. Dr. Arline C. Schmeer has shared with me the present state of her very exciting investigation into the possibility that clams will help us treat cancer. Many friends on Shelter Island have provided me with lore and recipes, and I especially thank "Captain" Frank Beckwith, who shared his own fifty years of experience on Shelter Island including his role as an officer of the Bayman's Association. Assistance with recipes has come from several good friends, including Libby Heineman and Camille Mastrogiovanni.

Don Allen, of New York and Shelter Island, was extremely supportive in planning and taking the cover photograph out on Shelter Island. My daughter Suzanne has been both patient with my demands and creative, indeed inspired, in working through the requirements of her wonderful illustrations. My other daughter Katharine has steadily and enthusiastically provided me with moral support, as has my wife, Mary K., whose editing pencil has been used here many times, and Jonas Zdanys, friend, Yale colleague, and fellow writer who regularly has urged me to keep writing. Paul Bradley and Martha Goldstein have been ideal literary agents, showing a sincere and committed interest from the very conception of this book. Peter Burford and Nick Lyons have been thoroughly supportive and understanding all the way, and Peter's editorial strength and practical judgment have been truly outstanding. All in all, then, this book comes with the support of many friends and I hope they will take some pleasure in knowing they made the following pages possible.

1.
Clams and Clamming

Man has been clamming since before recorded history. Long before he developed nets, hooks, lures, spears, shovels, forks, rakes, and other fishing and clamming tools, he simply used his hands and feet to find and dig clams. When fish and clams were both available to early man, he went either exclusively or initially for the clams. They are easier to catch. No less than our forebears, we continue to find satisfaction in harvesting food from the sea in such elemental ways. There is nothing difficult or mysterious about finding, gathering, opening, and preparing clams and other shellfish. The basic skills are easily learned. Clamming offers a uniquely direct form of physical contact with marine life, and awakens deep instinctual feelings we share as a species that likes to hunt.

I have been lucky to learn my clamming on Shelter Island, where the wind can always be heard in the rigging. Settled by whites in 1652, Shelter Island, which sits at the east end of the fork of Long Island and was known as "Ahaquatowamock" by the Indians, has abundant wildlife, a diverse set of beautiful shorelines, five harbors, and numerous tide creeks and tributaries. All islands, whether real or imagined such as Atlantis and Utopia, are metaphors for independence, and being marooned on an island is one of the great fantasies of literature and art. When I go searching for clams I think about the ways I am a part of a heritage of man's often lonely encounters with the sea, and of the challenge we associate with being on an island, cut off from the larger world but still able to find the food we need to survive.

A few weeks before I began to write this book I sat on a deserted stretch of beach and observed terns diving for fish. About thirty terns were working a two-hundred-yard section of water. They flapped, glided, and swooped back and forth closely parallel to the shore. When a tern spotted a fish it would turn to face the shore, maintain itself in a fixed position in space, beat its wings rapidly, and then dive straight down like a thunderbolt hurled by Zeus to catch the shining fish, which I could see in a bright flash as the tern swallowed and glided back into hunting. I could see each of the steps of the process simultaneously—some terns were diving while others rose, some swallowing while others positioned themselves for the dive, as still others cruised up and down, searching their next target.

I was struck by the terns' symphonic efficiency and smoothness as they hunted. Every tern caught a fish on every dive, and the one time I saw one drop its quarry, another tern, flying by below, immediately nailed it in midair. The terns have a system that works, that maximizes their understanding of when and where they will be able to catch the fish they need. Observing these beautiful birds made my principal goal in this book come clear—to convey a sense of "doing it right," to explain that there are time-proven ways to gather clams efficiently and to do so in harmony with nature. This analogy between the clamming of man and the fishing of terns is one that I have tried to make implicit throughout the book. The terns' behavior well illustrates my conviction that there is an intersection of aesthetic grace and practical efficiency that, ideally, characterizes any art. The art of clamming is no exception.

While there are some fifty or so kinds of regularly eaten clams around the world, my focus is on the principal ones gathered throughout the year by Amer-

Common terns.

icans. This country's coastal waters and tidal inlands are rich in clams, and although my experience has been on the East Coast, most of what I have learned about digging and raking clams can be put to equally good use on the West Coast and indeed all coasts. Therefore I have included, as an Appendix, a listing of the appropriate shellfish regulatory agency for every coastal state.

At the outset, let me dispel two popular myths about clams and clamming. First, with regard to clams: while it is true that you can become ill if you eat a clam taken from a highly polluted environment, that kind of area is "off limits." As long as you gather your clams, and other shellfish, in "safe" waters, they will be fine. In the Appendix, I direct you how to check on the waters of all the United States' coastal states. *Most* clams are *fine*. Approached as directed here, you will have good eating.

Second, while some shellfish, such as scallops, often can only legally be gathered in months that have an "r" in them (from September through April), *clams* can be gathered year-round. The "months with an 'r' in them" rule only tells you when scallops will be legally available. It is *not* talking about when shellfish are safe to eat. Clams can be eaten any month of the year, "r" or no "r."

For me, the activity of clamming is made more meaningful by knowing more about them, knowing their place in the biological world, knowing what kinds of references are made to them and how they are approached by people interested in such diverse fields as literature, history, archeology, and the sciences. The clam you hold casually in your hand is one of the most thoroughly researched animals in the world, and I think it makes clamming more engaging when you have a sense of the rich diversity of interest that surrounds them. My enjoyment of clamming is enhanced not only by the physical act of gathering them, but by steadily expanding my knowledge of what has been said or discovered about them.

To begin with, I think the word "clam" itself is interesting in both its derivation and its many uses. "Clam" is an Anglo-Saxon word that means, specifically, bond or fetter, but generally something closed tight, and appears with this usage in *Beowulf*, The German word "klamm" means "close," and the word "klammer" means not only a "clamp" but "parentheses." (When you enclose something in parentheses, you are clamming it up, and the marks certainly appear symetrically as linear bivalves.) The word "clam" has some other interesting things about it—it relates to clamor, which as a verb means to quiet or stop. In Scotland, to "clamjaffrey" means "to crowd," while "clamcrackers" are stingrays on the West Coast that feed, of all insult, on shellfish! And from Clam Falls, Wisconsin, to Clam River, Michigan, to Clam Harbor in Nova Scotia, clams are a proud part of geography. In slang, the word "clam" has been used variously—sometimes meaning someone who can keep a secret, as when a character in an early Ellery Queen novel exclaims, "I'm the original clam," or meaning a dollar, as when in John O'Hara's *Pal Joey* the pronouncement is made, "I hit a crap game for about eighty clams." Sometimes a clam means a goof or an error.

Clams have played their part in history, not only in this country but throughout the world. Paleolithic man used shells to make jewelry. The sharp edges of clams and other bivalves made them perfect cutting tools. In 35,000 B.C. or earlier, shells were used for working wood in places like Africa and Chile. American Indians frequently lashed surf clams to wooden sticks for use as hoes to prepare the ground for planting corn. They also used clam and whelk shells to make "wampum," a kind of money in which the scarcer fragments of purple shell were worth more than the white pieces. Archeologists have learned a great deal about prehistoric man by examining the "middens," or large piles of shells he discarded after eating. And as different shells have turned up in different parts of the world, we have used them to learn about primitive man's trading, eating, and traveling habits.

As the subject of scientific research, clams are extraordinary. One of the most impressive research areas is the investigation of the clam's potential for solving the age-old problem of cancer. Dr. Arline C. Schmeer, a Dominican sister now conducting her research at Saint Raphael's Hospital in New Haven, Connecticut, discovered in the 1960s that marine invertebrates rarely develop tumors. She was actually looking for a low-cost specimen with a tumor to use in her research into cancer. After being unable to find any clams with tumors, she began experimenting with extracts to look for anti-cancer agents. She has now developed a new substance she has named "Mercenene," a powerful anti-cancer agent, which she extracts from quahogs' livers. As we go to press she tells me

5

that she is entering the large-animal experiment stage, having treated tumors with total success in smaller animals. She has completed about two-thirds of the federal government's testing for possible toxic effects and has found absolutely none. The substance and the process for extracting it have both been registered with the government, and scientists around the world are watching and waiting to see if two or three years from now the possible miracle anti-cancer drug will be ready. It also is clear that the substance is effective in combatting bacteria and viruses.

I find it interesting to be aware not only of research into clams themselves and their possible medical uses, but to know about somewhat exotic-seeming kinds of research taking place all over the world, some of which relies on clams as a kind of partner. Just as one example, consider what recently occurred in the Saldanha Bay on the west coast of South Africa.

Researchers gathered clams in the Langebaan Lagoon and placed them in aquariums with different iron contents. After various manipulations and changes in the iron concentration, scientists used atomic absorption spectrophotometry to determine the iron content of the clams after first drying them out and rinsing them in nitric water. What they learned, happily, was that clams are an *excellent* tool for monitoring the change in the water's iron content, and therefore if there *were* to be excessive amounts in the Saldanha Bay and tidal currents were to carry the suspended iron into Langebaan Lagoon, the clams there would automatically serve as perfect and immediate indicators. Such exciting kinds of research activities that involve clams, as well as mussels and oysters, as biological "control agents" are increasing rapidly.

To illustrate a bit further the breadth of research presently taking place on clams, consider the following. Clam and scallop studies are being carried out in the Gulf of Mexico. Studies are being made to determine how to reduce winter mortalities of quahogs in Maine waters, how to protect seed clams from predators, on the effects of synthetic surfactants on the larvae of clams, on the predation of clams by crabs, on the effects of the Maryland soft-shelled clam industry on tidewater resources, and on the abundance and growth of clams in relationship to the character of different bottom sediments. Recently one researcher gathered oysters in Tasmania, Australia, kept them for a period of four months, then shipped them live to a colleague in Aberdeen, Scotland, who proceeded to kill them and expose treated tissue samples to the most sophisticated kinds of electron microscope and X-ray microanalysis available. The result was that some new things were learned about the oysters' kidneys, information which in turn may advance those who farm them commercially.

From Dr. Schmeer's cancer research, now making use of quahogs shipped almost frozen from Tampa Bay, to experiments in Africa and Australia, the clam is increasingly in the scientific spotlight.

Having an appreciation of the scientific community's interest in clams is well paralleled by developing a heightened sensitivity to the beauty of most clamming environments. While you don't clam at the same big beach where the waves are breaking and the surfers cruising, but instead in the inland waters, the bays and estuaries and tidal creeks, these calmer waters and shorelines are filled with their own evocative drama and power.

Clamming is more than something you do. It is something you *experience.* Standing alone at the edge of the water on a long stretch of beach, or walking slowly through an inland saltwater marsh at low tide, I feel very much in touch with nature and with an unchanging part of the world. Clamming brings you into a tranquility and sense of beauty in place that is hard to match. When you are clamming, you know you are doing something that others are doing around the world, that others have done for centuries upon centuries, and that generations will continue to do into the distant future.

Consider, just for a moment, some of the rich imagery that surrounds you on a typical clam outing. Seaweed has been pushed by the tide and the wind high onto the shore in twisted, disconnected strands and bundles. Small fragments of painted and worn wood are trapped in matted dead sea grasses strung parallel to the shore. A dry, empty black skate egg case partly covered by baby mussels rests beside the miniature baby carriages of bleached limpet shells. The sun catches bits of bright quartz and scallop shell edges, while swallows dip in

Skate egg case.

and out of the grasses. Out in the water a loon goes under while across the way above land an osprey teaches its young to fly. When I walk along one of my favorite clamming shores, I pass by a dead horseshoe crab, upside down, its last few legs uneaten, but pick up a piece of rope attached to a plastic bottle, both covered with large beautiful barnacles. Returning, I pass tangled white nylon nets with thicker, braided turquoise rope snaking through it, piles of nets with large beaded brown corks like so many baked apples. Feathers, conch shells cradled in matted grass, bits of smooth glass, bleached spider crab claws, oak leaves from distant trees—the list is endless, the setting overwhelming in its variety.

THE BIOLOGY OF CLAMS

There are five "kingdoms" of life: 1) *Prokaryota* (viruses, bacteria, etc); 2) *Protista* (includes *Protophyta* and *Protozoa*); 3) *Fungi*; 4) *Metaphyta (Plantae)*, which includes all other plants; and 5) *Metazoa (Animalia)*, which includes all other animals, including man and clams!

Within the *Metazoa* kingdom there are many different groups, each known as a phylum, and clams are in the phylum known as *Mollusca*. The phylum

Mollusca, which Aristotle used originally to designate a group mostly of cuttlefish, eventually grew to include an enormous variety of creatures that live all over the world, ranging in size from the giant squid, with a forty foot armspan, to the tiniest snail only a millimeter in length.

Mollusks derive their name from the Latin word "mollis," which means "soft," which is the key to what they all have in common. Whether blue sea slugs, clams, snails, or squid, mollusks have a soft body and no internal skeleton. All have a slippery, mucus-secreting skin, and most, but not literally every species, also have an external calcareous shell. Some mollusks have a shell that actually grows inside their bodies, as for example the "pen" in squids (so named because it resembles the old-fashioned quill pen) or the "cuttlebone" in cuttlefish. Mollusks live all over the world, and in all kinds of places, from deserts to mountain tops, but all must keep their bodies wet to stay alive.

At this writing there are some 110,000 known kinds of living mollusks, and as someone who has sat on the shores of Loch Ness looking for the monster, I, for one, believe that there are probably as many more that we don't know about yet. In 1966 only forty thousand living species were known. And we do know that at least forty thousand more kinds of mollusks once existed and are now extinct. With as many extinct (but captured in fossil records) as are known alive, it is not unlikely to believe that something more spectacular than the octopus or more delicious than a soft-shelled clam still remains to be discovered. I have seen estimates that about one thousand new mollusks are being discovered each year.

Mollusks are grouped into six or seven classes, but most experts concentrate on the four principal ones: (1) *Polyplacophora* (also known as *Loricata*); (2) *Gastropoda;* (3) *Bivalvia* (also known as *Pelecypoda*); and (4) *Cephalopoda.*

Our interest is in the Bivalves, or Pelecypods (derived from the Greek words "pelekys," meaning hatchet, and "pous," or foot because of the bivalves' strong hatchet-shaped foot). Bivalves, all of which are aquatic and 80 percent of which live in salt water, are the second largest class of mollusks (gastropods are the largest and are all univalves, while the octopuses, squids, and others of the cephalopods are the most active). Within the class of *Bivalvia* there is a particular subclass known as *Lamellibranchia*. All of its members, including clams, have two adductor muscles, generally of equal size. Oysters, scallops, and mussels are in the subclass order, *Anisomyaria*. Members of this group have an enlarged posterior muscle near the center of the shell and the anterior muscle is either small or non-existent.

All bivalves have two symmetrical shells that are hinged together along the upper midline. These two shells are generally open to some degree as the creatures feed, but are pulled closed when the creatures are threatened. Though they have differences in their traveling patterns, clams hold their two valves together with two adductor muscles, one on the anterior end and one on the posterior end (mussels have one large posterior and one small anterior adductor muscle, while both scallops and oysters have just a single muscle). A bivalve that never completely closes, like the steamer, razor clam, or geoduck is said to be "gaping." Most bivalves use their foot to burrow or escape; the foot is extended, hooks into the sand or mud, then pulls its body toward it in a series of motions. An exception is the razor clam, which uses its foot not to pull itself forward or down in a series of jerks, but instead to dig a full hole, after which it contracts and pulls its shell very rapidly down into it in a smooth motion, traveling its body length in about six seconds.

All bivalves are either burrowing and moving around or are instead attached by byssus threads, bundles of protein fibers, to other objects that are often stationary. There are some fifteen thousand kinds of bivalves. Some burrow many feet beneath the ocean floor, whereas others, like the scallop, sometimes swim freely and frolic in the waves. Bivalves come in various shapes, but all hold their shells together by either one or two adductor muscles. In every bivalve, the two shells and the ligament that hinges them are secreted by the mantle, or fleshy outer section of the outside wall of the clam's softer body.

Since we like to eat clams, it is only fair that we should know how *they* eat, which is a rather extraordinary process. Clams, like all bivalves, eat the plankton—microscopic plants and animals—in the water that surrounds them.

Every day huge amounts of planktonic food rise from the ocean's depths to the surface as sunset approaches and then descend when the light returns at daybreak. Many predators, including clams, adjust their feeding schedules to this endless rhythm of the sea, thereby creating a choreography driven by changes in light.

Clams bring in water containing planktonic food through one siphon (the aptly named inhalant syphon), letting it pass over their gills where mucus strands catch the microscopic particles and push them toward their single mouth, and then use little whiskbroom "pulps" to push the food into the esophagus. Then their other, or exhalant, siphon sends the water, now stripped of its nourishing food, back out. Many bivalves turn over hundreds of gallons of water daily in this way, and all of them bring enough water in and out to meet their food needs. In different bivalves, the inhaling and exhaling siphons take different forms (see, for example, the jacknife clam, p.34).

All animals reproduce at some point in their life cycle and clams are no exception. They reproduce sexually. There are males and females, and although the sexes are usually separate, some hermaphrodites exist. Some bivalves change sex, first developing male sex organs only to have them replaced by female ones. Clam eggs are generally fertilized outside the body, but a few clams keep them inside. There are no external indications of sex on bivalve shells, so for all practical purposes, you don't know, or need to, whether you have dug up a male or a female. Once fertilized, clam eggs have a blissful free-swimming period, but then they ultimately settle down and stay on the bottom. They may settle in sandy or muddy bottoms, in loose quartz sand, white sand, shell and sea grass combinations, substrates containing mud and rock, or—they adapt to whatever characteristics they find on the sea floor. They appear most often in sandy and muddy bay and estuary bottoms.

Hard-shelled clams move around quite a bit, but soft-shelled clams generally just move vertically (an adaptative ability to escape predators, including man) and thus spend the bulk of their life in approximately the same area. *This distinction in habits will have significant importance to your clamming strategies.*

Hardshell clam.

The principal soft-shelled clam, or "steamer," is the *Mya arenaria*. The principal hard-shelled clam, the quahog or chowder clam, exists in both a northern and southern variety. The southern quahog, which is found from New Jersey south to Florida and the Gulf of Mexico, is known as *Mercenaria campechiensis;* the northern quahog, which is closely related, and which lives inshore from the southern quahog where it is found and exists all the way up to the Gulf of the St. Lawrence, is known as *Mercenaria mercenaria,* and even more typically as *Venus mercenaria.* (The Latin name prompted Dr. Schmeer to name her anticancer substance "Mercenene".)

The common or eastern oyster we will be talking about is known as *Crassostrea virginica,* the common Atlantic bay scallop is *Aequipecten irradians,* and I will also discuss the blue mussel, quite familiar because commercially harvested and served in restaurants, known as *Mytilus edulis;* the ribbed mussel, *Ischadium demissum,* is a delicious variety that relatively few people know about.

In addition to knowing about the place of clams and other bivalves in the natural world, it is useful to be cognizant of the large-scale commercial farming or aquaculture work that is taking place around the world. Mechanical shellfish harvesting may seem incompatible with our solitary clamming outings, but the commercial activities frequently generate significant useful research that redounds to the benefit of shellfish, just as baymen's associations take up environmental issues in ways that protect us all. There is not, therefore, any necessary rivalry between commercial and individual shellfishing. The two are part of a shared food-harvesting process that goes back millions of years, and in fact we know through fossil records that clams go back at least six hundred million years.

In succeeding chapters I will share with you everything I have learned about clamming. I do so knowing that there is much that I still have to learn. I have also found, sometimes unfortunately, that there are other beachcombers who are quick to offer unrequested advice about how to do things better, and undoubtedly you will run into these individuals yourself. I always try to keep in mind Aesop's fable of "The Mice in Council." This is the story of a group of mice who gather behind closed doors to decide what measures they can take to reduce the dangerous threat of the Cat. A young mouse gives a rousing speech proposing that the answer is simple, that they should put a bell around the cat's neck so they will be warned if it comes near. A motion is passed to vote praise for the young mouse, and to adopt his idea, but the old mouse, who has been sitting and listening quietly, says that before the praise is voted, he would like the young mouse to explain how the bell is going to be put around the cat's neck and who is going to put it there. As Aesop notes in his follow-up application, "many things appear sensible in speculation, which are afterwards found to be impracticable." So when I am given advice about clamming from people whose suggestions are of dubious merit, I usually mumble, "And who's going to bell the cat?" It's worth remembering!

Another important point to keep in mind as you prepare for clamming is that it must be undertaken with a keen respect for the environment. The clamming industry is periodically under seige from man's inattention to ecological factors, and every individual clammer must do his or her part to protect clams in addition to enjoying them. This means that the first rule of clamming is to obey its laws. Get to know the shellfish rules and regulations in your area.

Although in general it is wisest to talk with local authorities, you also should—particularly if you are going to clam in a state for the first time—write to the state environmental agency that oversees shellfishing laws. A listing of coastal state offices and addresses is included in the Appendix. Often you will need to get a shellfish permit from the town offices, where you will be given rules, just as with many fishing licenses, stipulating the size allowed and the daily quota. It might be typical, for example, that steamers cannot be taken under two inches in length or in more than one peck in a day. Which, if you are hungry, is why it makes sense to plan a clamming trip so you will be able to gather oysters and mussels as well as both hard-shelled and soft-shelled clams. Such multipurpose outings are an especially good way to prepare for a clambake (see p.113).

This book is by no means encylopedic. I have tried to assimilate the views of others, as well as the factual, verifiable kinds of information available in a wide set of resource and reference works. But the thrust of the "how-to" information must, of necessity, flow from my personal experiences, biases, and opinions. There are others, I am sure, who know more about clamming than I do, but that sort of statement is one that authors turning toward any subject can usually make and therefore I offer no apology. Clamming, as an art and as a life experience, is at the center of my being, and it not only brings me but keeps me in touch with myself. I am, like many other clammers, I suspect, a bit compulsive about it, finding that each time I bring a clam up I want to go back and

14

get "just one more." There is an old German legend about a monk living in Hildesheim who doubted that a thousand years with God could only be, as some people expressed it, but a single day. So the monk happily listens for three minutes to the melody of the bird, only to learn later that he had been listening to it for a hundred years. It is with this sense of time being perceived enthusiastically that I turn to steamers, leaving *my* birds, the terns, whose beauty and efficiency served as my point of departure.

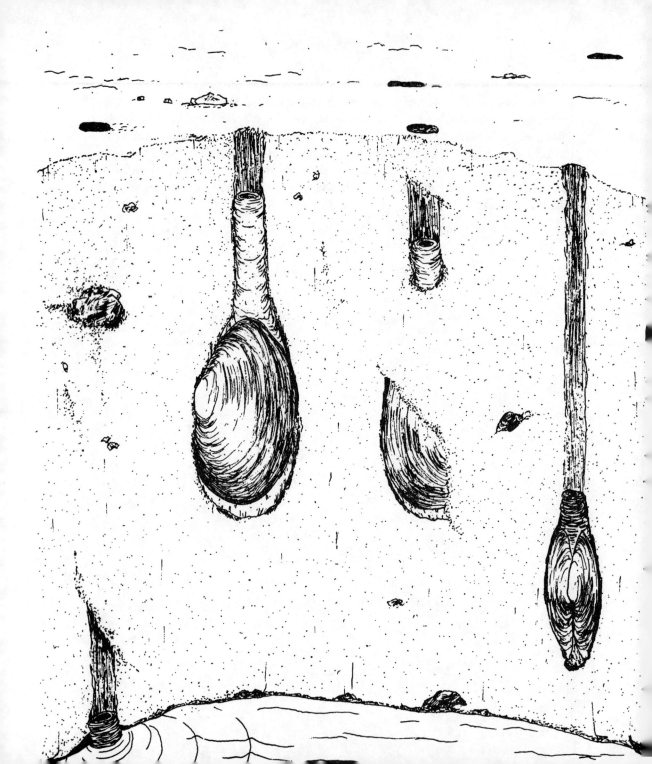

2.
Softshell Clams

The soft-shelled clam of principal interest to us is the feisty and dramatic "steamer" (*Mya arenaria*, often simply referred to as the *Mya*). It lives primarily in the intertidal zone, moves vertically in the sand and mud with a very strong foot, and brings water loaded with microscopic food in and out of its body with particularly long siphons enclosed in a rubbery tube. The steamer has acquired a distinctively "gamey" personality because of its keen ability to sense danger and to dig down to escape predators. Its unique taste makes it more than a worthy catch, and ducks, swans, raccoons, and even some rays share our enthusiasm for catching and eating it. Along both the Atlantic and Pacific coasts, it's a favorite seafood, and for polar bears in the Arctic, it's a gourmet item. Seals get their fair share as well.

Although some steamers live below the tide line (subtidally), most are above it, and represent the ones you will dig, whether you search out on the "flats" of muddy surfaces or along relatively narrow sandy shorelines. Steamers have oval valves marked with concentric rings that give them a slightly ridged feeling. They range in color from white to bluish gray. Also known as the Long Neck Clam (because of the long, leathery, tubelike epidermis containing its two siphons and which is called its "neck," even though it isn't, for its head is at the opposite end), as the Gaper, the Nannynose, or the "piss clam," the steamer is a burrowing bivalve that eats with its "neck" extended so that its two siphons can inhale and exhale the food-bearing water; this neck contracts when the steamer senses predation, thereby giving off a squirt of water, sometimes in a quick short squirt and other times in a long-drawn-out fountain, though its siphons can be seen through the gaping open posterior end even when contracted.

In Shakespeare's *Julius Caesar* we find the famous lines:

> *There is a tide in the affairs of men,*
> *Which, taken at the flood, leads on to fortune;*
> *Omitted, all the voyage of their life*
> *Is bound in shallows and in miseries (IV, iii)*

When it comes to gathering steamers, however, Shakespeare's advice must be put aside. You make *your* fortune at low tide.

Steamer (softshell clam).

Because steamers must be gathered at low tide, and because it is virtually impossible to gather them under water, it is essential to understand what tides are and how they work. The tide is our term for the falling and the rising of the ocean that results from the attraction between the sun and the moon. As well summarized by Willard Bascom, "On all seacoasts there is a rhythmic rise and fall of the water which is called the tide, and associated with this vertical movement of the water surface are horizontal motions of the water known as tidal currents. Together they are known as tides." (*Waves and Beaches: The Dynamics of the Ocean Surface*, New York, 1962, p. 82). Tides "work" somewhat differently in different parts of the world. In parts of the Gulf of Mexico and the Pacific Ocean, there is only one tide change each day. In Tahiti the high tide arrives at exactly the same time each day. In general, however, and all along the Atlantic and Pacific coasts of America, low tide, that point at which the water has receded from the shore as far as it can, occurs approximately twelve hours and forty minutes after the preceding low tide. The high tide, that point when the water has risen as high as it ever does onto the land, also occurs at this same interval.

Expressed differently, low tide follows high tide by just over six hours, and the times of each advance about forty minutes each day. If low tide is at six P.M. on Monday, it will be at about six-forty P.M. on Tuesday. This pattern is known as "tidal oscillation," and it takes place with complete predictability, making it easy to plan steamer gathering at the most opportune time. While you can make general plans for catching salt-water fish in certain areas on an incoming tide or an outgoing tide, with *clams* you can plan with total accuracy because they are going to be particularly vulnerable *at* a known time for a predictable *amount* of time. Some tides operate a bit strangely, nevertheless, and legend has it that Aristotle, when he was quite old, died of despair that he could not explain the phenomenon of a particular Greek channel's tide changing every three hours, a phenomenon which, by the way, has not yet been explained. In the spring, when the moon is full, you have "perigee tide high and perigee tide low," meaning larger variations in both the high tide and the

Tides.

low tide. Smaller variations, in reverse, occur when the moon is small, and are known as "neap" tides. Thus when you go for steamers in the spring, you have access to some large steamers that in the summer are typically under more water.

Steamers live in the sand and mud along the edges of beaches and salt marshes from Labrador to North Carolina on the Atlantic coast and from California to Alaska on the Pacific. They burrow into the sand or mud and live there throughout both high and low tide. Since they are sitting there feeding, we can make good use of our understanding of the tides to gather them. The ocean is always moving, and the tide is always coming in or out, even if, as in the Mediterranean Sea, with only minimal change of sea level. Connecticut is really the Indian word "Quonoktacut," meaning a river whose water is powered and altered by the tides and the wind. The very slowest movement of the water takes place in the last twenty minutes it is going out and during the first twenty minutes it is starting to "turn around" and come back in. *This forty-minute period of slowest movement, known as "slack tide," provides you with your most opportune period in which to dig steamers, particularly in the area closest to the tide line, where they are frequently the most abundant.*

When low tide occurs—typically a drop of a few feet, but less than a foot in some places and over forty feet in the Bay of Fundy—the steamers' presence can be detected, to some extent but by no means exclusively, by small holes in which their elongated "necks" are resting. When you walk along the water's edge at low tide you will often see small holes of different sizes and occasionally you will see a squirt of water flying up, an indication that the steamer is trying to avoid you because it guesses, rightly, that you are a predator.

The hole in the sand made by the steamer is smaller than certain other holes you see, especially those made by the fiddler crab, usually the sand fiddler. These holes tend to be about three times as large as the steamer holes, which are usually about a quarter of an inch in diameter. As the male fiddler crab eats,

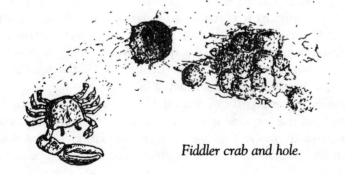

Fiddler crab and hole.

21

he makes small balls of sand with his pincer and pushes them out, thereby creating holes. These sand balls sit on the surface like miniature billiard balls, and their presence immediately adjacent to holes confirms the presence of fiddler crabs. It is unwise to be too curious and stick your finger in one of these holes, inasmuch as the oversized pincer, used as a courtship device, is not something you want clamping onto your finger.

When steamers are covered by the tidal waters flowing above the sand, they are busily eating. When the tide recedes and they are unable to bring the water "down" to them, steamers are simply stationary. Most rest their shell-enclosed bodies from three to nine inches below the surface. Although they prefer to settle in relatively soft sand and mud, they also appear in rocky areas and in sand heavily mixed with rocks and broken shells.

To dig steamers you need to have a pail that will hold several gallons of water, allowing you to keep your catch fresh, and one of the following: a *pointed* spade or shovel (either long-handled or short-handled), a pitchfork, or a short-handled clam rake that looks like a pitchfork whose tongs have been bent to a ninety-degree angle, but lacks the basket of the long-handled clam rake that you use to gather hard-shelled clams. Since you can use only one of them at a time, you may want to experiment with all of them. My preference is for a pointed spade because I find it turns up the first batch of mud or sand in a very neat and clean way. Also, in looser sand, a pitchfork doesn't turn it over fully. If you are in the generally harder mud of clam flats, you will keep using your instrument more vigorously, as it is harder to separate the tightly packed mud with your hands. If it is cold, you will want to use your hands relatively little, wear gloves, and keep turning the mud or sand with your shovel, fork, or short-handled rake. In the summer you can wear sneakers or, if the area is free of debris, go barefoot; if it is cold, wear insulated boots.

Because steamers live primarily in the intertidal zone, that surface area of shore that extends from the low tide to the high tide water movement, the best places to look for them are where that zone is relatively large. Thus it is usually productive to search out some "flats," or expansive flat areas of muddy bottom

Steamer rake (short handled).

that are fully uncovered with water during low tide. But the flats should not be your only location. You can find good clamming spots in virtually any kind of shoreline setting, but along the edges of coves and wide-mouthed inlets you are apt to do well. The second specific thing to look for after large intertidal space is relatively soft sand or mud. Since steamers burrow down, it stands to reason that they can do that most easily in soft textures. But again, don't let that set limits on your explorations, as they can and do burrow in much harder bottoms.

Steamers usually make holes that are not always visible, nor are they always large. As often as not, *you* will induce the steamer suddenly to make a hole by hitting the sand or mud with your shovel or fork or by stomping on the surface. By alarming the steamer, you force it into the sudden contraction that sends up the water and opens up a hole. If you are clamming in coarser sand

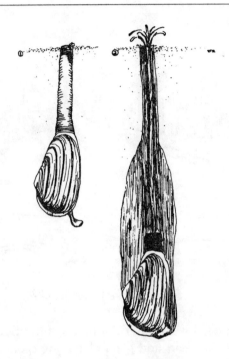

Steamer escaping predation.

mixed in with many rocks, there is simply no way for the holes to show up very clearly, even though the steamer has exhaled water. Therefore you should look for slight dark shadowlike openings adjacent to rocks, or even cracks of air between rocks, to discover the steamer's presence. Beneath rocks, the steamer's exhaled water is more widely dispersed.

If you are walking along the tide line at low tide and not seeing any holes, try tapping your shovel or fork lightly against the bottom just below the water. Often this will result in seeing some large holes open up beneath the water. This means that the tide is either not quite dead low or, at that time of year in that location, the steamers are covered with slightly more water. If you dig down hard underneath one of these large dark holes, you will probably come up each time with one or two steamers, but because you are under water, you cannot create a hole and dig farther into it. Getting one at a time is okay, especially if they are of good size. The point is to keep looking even if you don't see holes or squirts. Steamers often need to be stimulated into the creation of holes. It is also quite typical to begin digging under one hole and find a number of other holes suddenly appearing, much as a pancake indicates it is ready to be turned.

Steamers have relatively brittle shells and thus you should handle them carefully. The average mature steamer is about two and a half or three inches long, but they can be found up to four or five inches, particularly in the winter months when tides are lower and provide access to steamers exposed to the air for only a short time.

By arriving a half hour or more before low tide, you have time to hunt and explore before beginning to dig at the ideal, slack-tide time. You should always begin by digging as close to the water's edge as possible, for soon the incoming water will arrive and cover the clams, making them much less accessible. Then you can gradually move higher onto the shore to the next level of clams. When those are under water, move up again. If for some reason you arrive quite a bit *before* low tide, which will be evident as the water continues to recede, keep following the tide line lower, moving toward the newly exposed shore area. (I always mark, with a stone or piece of driftwood, the edge of the tide line so I can be certain, after awhile, that the tide is in fact still going out.)

Like many other bivalves, particularly oysters, steamers tend to live in colonies, and thus you are likely to encounter groups of them. If, however, you see a *very* large number of relatively small holes together, say only an inch apart, the density is likely to be such that the clams beneath are still much too young and are therefore small enough to be tightly crowded together. Keep walking until you find holes that are relatively numerous but have some space between them. And remember, the bigger steamers almost always are as close to the tide line as you can dig; if the mud is quite solid, you can even just rapidly turn one shovelful after another right on the tide line. It is generally wiser, in any case, to walk farther than you might choose to at first; in this way you increase the likelihood of finding a spot less explored by others.

Steamers are tenacious when they dig down. First, the foot they use for burrowing extends, while the siphons that are on the other, upside, end are also extended. The siphons are pulled in, the adductor muscle contracts, and the water in the mantle cavity is compressed and then ejected out the pedal gape surrounding the extended foot with such force that it loosens the bottom or sand, allowing the foot immediately to move down. As blood rushes into the foot, from the same contraction movement, it becomes strong and hooks like an anchor, pulling the body farther down. Then the siphons are extended again and the same burrowing motion is repeated. It's a tough and quick display of independence, and the speed at which steamers descend is remarkable. Fortunately there are ways to take advantage of their predictable flight response in a real game of cat and mouse.

A clamming outing needs to be thought through, so I will describe a typical outing. I walk along the tide line, passing the first steamer holes I see. I've clammed these spots before, and so have other clammers. I look for signs of recent clamming activity in the form of mounds in the sand not fully leveled out by the water. I enjoy observing snowy egrets carefully placing one foot in front of the other as they stalk fish in the very shallow water in the grasses. I check out beds of mussels. I look for signs of oysters.

When I go after steamers, in the late spring or summer, I like to wear a ratty old pair of sneakers. I don't think there's a saltwater creek anywhere that doesn't conceal a sharp shell, a tin-can lid, a broken bottle, or a rusty rough piece of metal. Sneakers are good friends against the unseen.

There are a number of ways to get steamers out of the sand. I know someone who backs his outboard motor into a soft, muddy shore bank and blows the clams out of their holes. But let's talk about the *right* way. Once you have selected a promising place, defined as one where you see either one or several surface holes several inches apart, position yourself as close as possible to the water's edge. Face the shore and dig a hole in the sand by placing either a pointed shovel, a pitchfork, or a short-handled clam rake straight down to the hilt slightly downshore from the clam hole (about four to five inches away from the hole so you avoid actually hitting the steamer), and then lift your first shovelful out. Leave a foot or more of space between the hole and the water's edge, as you do not want the hole to fill up too rapidly with water. The trick is to get some, but not too much, water into the hole and use it as an accomplice to help weaken or erode the harder, more compacted sand or mud. Do not worry about what you might have dug up in your shovel; just leave it in the shovel for the time being. That shovelful of sand or mud is not going anywhere, but your intrusion has already set all the clams in the immediate area into a frenzy of escape. You have to get them before they are out of reach.

With your hands, widen the hole with a circular motion, digging with your fingers against the sandy sides, using the water to make the sides of the hole cave in every so often. This usually reveals steamers suspended vertically, next to one another, their siphons either contracting or about to contract. Always grab for the ones most out of sight, sometimes simply visible from the tops of their black necks.

Steamer digging.

Pull the steamers out of the loosened sand or mud by grabbing them firmly even as they are trying to dig down. When your eye spots a steamer going down, move very quickly just to get a finger or two into contact with it, and *don't lose that contact or else it will be out of sight and reach before you know it.* Then run your finger carefully but firmly down along either of its flat shells on the *side* (not along the gaping *edges* which can cut you), and stay with it as it travels down farther, all the time applying some pressure to make it pitch forward into the hole, which, if you are relatively near the water, will be slowly filling with water.

As you work the hole with your hands, keep your eye out along the sides at all times, and keep grabbing one whenever you see it. If you are finding them every so often, you can place each one you catch on the surface nearby. If you are finding lots of steamers, don't take the time to place them aside but simply knock them into the hole, then periodically scoop out a bunch at once. Remember the swift efficiency of the terns. If you find several adjacent steamers, as is common, try not only to keep a finger or two in contact with one as it descends but simultaneously to use several other fingers of the same hand to exert light pressure against the sand or mud surrounding those nearby. I generally use one hand this way and the other hand to swirl water around in the hole, sculpting the lower walls of the hole, creating the overhanging ledge, thereby exposing more clams or siphon tips for the other hand to move to. The more you can get several fingers low or under the steamer, the better, because you are interrupting its escape route. Remember, the harder it is for *you* to dig into the lower, harder mud or sand, the harder it also is for the steamer.

There is a chance to maximize your catch by using your hands in combinations of these activities: digging, pulling mud and sand apart, "staying with" a steamer once your fingers have made contact with it as it goes down, tossing some onto the sand, and swirling the water to loosen the sand or mud. Keep mixing these activities when you are into a thick bunch, and after some experience you will get a sense of how much time and motion should be devoted to each. If you are on thick mud flats and only finding one steamer every so often, you will then need to dig or turn over the mud with more rather than fewer repetitions. But if you see plenty, stay very active and exhaust each hole's supply. Keep watching for quick motions of the contracting tips of steamer necks and go right down next to them. Unlike dolphins, which as Audubon observed and described so well, gather sympathetically around one of their own when it is caught, steamers do everything to "distance" themselves when one of their neighbors is being nabbed.

When you dig your hole, keep working the circular edge in front of you, right around to the sides, thereby creating a circular overhanging "ledge." This allows you to see the steamers suspended vertically in the underside of the ledge and get them quite easily when you knock the ledge down. This gives you the advantage of surprise. When the ledge collapses, pull the dropped sand toward you immediately, thereby exposing steamers just before they start to dig hard. Don't be surprised if the steamers don't dig straight down but often a little sideways as well. You may even think you've lost the steamer, momentarily, but just keep digging. It is tempting, but usually futile, to try to grab the steamer from the top. You are always better off to run a finger or two down along its broad shell, then pry it toward you. Again, it is important not to let it out of *touch* even after it is out of sight.

Once you have exhausted the supply of steamers in one hole, begin another just far enough away so that the two holes won't "connect," which would result in letting in too much water at once. Incidentally, if you find a dead steamer in a hole, there is no need to think that you have come upon a polluted area. The live clams nearby are fine. If gnats are bothering you, keep rinsing your arms and legs in the water nearby. Gnats tend to make me work faster, which increases my efficiency. To dig steamers is to come to respect speed in execution, to believe, as John Masefield wrote, that "all the great things of life are swiftly done."

Don't try to get every steamer. A risk/reward situation applies here. Sometimes you have to allow a fast burrower to get away in order to get the three that are just beginning to descend. Some sacrifice is wise, though there are enthusiasts who will virtually throw themselves into the hole before allowing even one steamer to get away. In the eighteenth century, an "enthusiast" was a euphemism for someone deranged.

The clamming season is open throughout the year. Although most communities have restrictions on the number of clams a noncommercial clammer can gather each day, you can usually go and dig them no matter what the weather (those who wish to obtain a commercial clamming license will find that there are also set quotas). Obviously you have to curtail your clamming if you are in an area where the water becomes prohibitively cold, but even in this season you can still dig and, usually with rubber-gloved hands, pick some out. Certainly the commercial clammers who depend on digging clams for a living don't stop because the weather gets cold or it rains. In the spring when the tides run out farther, broader expanses of the intertidal area become exposed and you can usually do very well if you are willing to put up with the cold. And since you can usually get a pretty good supply in the "slack tide" period of about forty minutes, you can scurry home and get warm by the fire.

The best way to handle steamers as you dig them up is to take along a good-sized pail (a large plastic pail holding at least a few gallons and with a handle works fine). Essentially, you want the pail to be large enough so that it will be easy to carry with quite a few steamers and a lot of salt water without having the water splash all over your legs as you walk back with your catch. As I remove the clams from the hole, I simply put them in a pile on the surface of the sand near to where I am digging (but out of the line of the development of the larger hole, as you don't want any to fall in and disappear). When finished with one hole (it soon gets filled with water and turned sand or mud that makes it impracticable to continue), I take all the steamers in my pile into the water and wash them off, then put them in the pail. In this way, I don't unnecessarily put any loose sand into the pail, and the cleaner the water in the pail stays, the better.

Every so often you should take the pail and twist it by the handle back and forth vigorously, imitating an agitator in a washing machine. This will shake loose more sand. Then change the water by pouring it off while you hold the steamers in with your hand and dipping the pail back in the water several feet away from where you have dumped the old water. By taking these steps for just a few minutes during the course of the steamer-gathering outing, I am washing the steamers several times, and by giving them clean water to take into and out of their system as they sit in the pail, they are cleansing themselves as well. As I walk back along the shoreline, I usually stop, repeat the agitator movement, and replace the water several times.

By the time I get home the steamers are already well on their way to being clean. Some people put cornmeal in the pail of water when they get the steamers home. As the steamers digest some of this and exhale it, they remove some of their inside sand as well. But if you proceed as I have suggested from the time you actually dig the clams up, the clams will be well cleaned. Steamers will keep for a long time if they are simply placed in the refrigerator in a bowl. If after several days in the refrigerator the steamers seem somewhat unlively (their necks, for example, don't want to contract when you touch them), get a pail of seawater, place them in it, and they will revive quickly. If a steamer floats when you put it in water, it is dead and should not be eaten (this is true when you are digging them as well). In general, it is best to eat steamers within forty-eight hours after you dig them up.

I don't like to stop digging steamers too early. Partly this is because I enjoy them so much, but partly I simply like to prolong my encounter with the water and the ways it catches light. Clamming, remember, is an opportunity to discover things about yourself as a hunting animal, and there is an instinctual individuality about that. Accordingly, it is only fair to respect the privacy of others you see clamming. Thus, in general, don't begin to dig right on top of someone who has already started digging before you arrive. There is nothing wrong with clamming on the same stretch of beach where other clammers are working, and being friendly and indicating your shared purpose is fine, but nevertheless, don't crowd anyone.

Never carry steamers home in a dry pail. They will inevitably be sandy and

gritty. Don't clam without knowing the area's regulations and permit requirements. Don't force children to go if they are not really anxious to. Very young
children seem genuinely excited about clams and like to see them in their
natural habitat. Some kids, however (and you will know best if yours are in this
group), are at that age when they see clams in the same way that they see toads
and turtles, as objects of torture.

Don't discard a steamer whose shell you break. Just wash it off as best you
can and keep it with the others. It will taste just as good as long as you rinse it
fully. Don't keep any tiny clams. As with fish, they don't look any bigger when
you get them home. The general rule in most communities is two inches or
more in *shell* length. Don't leave tiny clams out on the surface—push them
back into the hole. They will never get larger if you don't help them.

I know it might seem trivial, but I see people every summer who come
down to the salt marshes to dig steamers and clams wearing clean white socks
and sneakers or shoes. They roll up their pants, if they are wearing them, and
proceed to cover their white socks with the black mud and sand that gets
kicked around and sloshed on them when they begin to get into a hole. Wear
old sneakers or, if your feet are fairly tough, you can go for steamers barefoot
(since when getting steamers you can see where you are stepping). The biggest
problem in going for steamers barefoot is that it is hard to press down on your
shovel or fork. As for socks, they are just not *de rigeur* from any point of view.

Digging steamers at different times of year poses different problems. In
most communities, you can go for any kind of clams all year long. In the early
spring, when the water is usually quite cold, you need to work even faster than
usual and take some breaks so that your hands can warm up, and you need to
rely a bit more on your shovel or pitchfork. In colder weather, you should wear
tall, heavy rubber boots since your feet will often be in water or at least exposed
to very cold air. Several layers of clothes help against the wind. In the warmer
months, the less you wear, the better. There is no point in taking a shirt or
windbreaker, as digging steamers can get pretty messy. Just wear a bathing suit,
and maybe a T-shirt. One of the nicest things about summer clamming is that

you can leave your shovel and basket on shore and just take a swim, get clean and refreshed, and then go back to clamming. No clam has been frightened away by a swimmer.

Insects can be a problem in the summer months when most steamer-digging by amateur clammers takes place. The life revealed by low tide tends to attract gnats and tiny fleas that will come right into the hole where you are digging. Out of the muck can come some pretty strong stenches, which turn on certain bugs. Tiny gnat bites will leave you covered with little red spots which will look larger by the time you get home, but disappear the following day. Green-eyed flies pose a greater problem. Everyone has a different way to cope with flies. I spread some black smelly mud on one of my calf muscles and let the flies land there—it's a good hard place to swat and kill them, and much pleasanter than slapping your face. Sometimes I break open a clam and smear it around on a nearby rock, pour a little water on it, and the flies find this more attractive than they do me. If I get really annoyed, I will go for a swim and hold my breath under water while the hungry and generally impatient flies go and find someone else. No doubt they particularly like my blood because I eat so many clams.

In general the individual clammer can get plenty of steamers in an hour or so. Then it is smart to try to add some mussels and oysters through some underwater searching. Steamers can form the foundation of a clamming outing, since they need to be dug at the very lowest tide, while the others can wait.

There also are other soft-shelled clams to be on the lookout for. In the northwest there is the geoduck *(Panope generosa)*, which is indeed very generous. It burrows up to two feet deep as it grows to full size, weighing ten to twelve pounds. And its shell, like that of other soft-shelled clams, is light in weight, so that's a lot of clam.

I'm a fan of the jackknife clam, known as *Tagelus plebeius,* and although it is used for bait on the West Coast, I have eaten them and, though a little sandy, have found them fine. The jackknife clam is well named, because its two short siphons stick out like the stubby blades of a pocket knife. Its shape and

Jacknife clam.

four-inch length make it feel like a Swiss army knife. I am most apt to find jackknife clams when I am digging cherrystones or quahogs. It is a deep burrower and, unlike the steamer, spends most of its time below the tide line. It likes the thicker mud and silt bottoms of bays and marshes, just as the short-siphoned hard-shelled clams do, and yet its taste and "gaping" nature make it an obvious close relation of the steamer. You can cook and eat them in the same way as steamers. Although they can be found from Cape Cod to Florida, they are generally not so abundant as steamers, and you are more likely to pick up only a few rather than dozens unless you are making a concerted effort to find them. I usually bring a few up in my rake, but not by hand (though I have, on occasion, found some in steamer holes).

The razor clam has a long muscular foot that allows it to burrow deeply and rapidly. When you dig steamers, you keep enlarging the hole and letting the side sand fall in as you explore the lower inside edges for the tips of the steamers' necks as they pull down. The razor clam doesn't allow you the same luxury of time because it is descending extremely rapidly, and the water coming into the hole further loosens the sand. Every so often razor clams are found lying on the surface (the same is occasionally true of quahogs), and then you can quickly grab them. They feel like the long opened razors for which they're named, and, because they are gaping, they too remind you immediately of steamers, perhaps as viewed through one of those funhouse mirrors that elongates everything.

Razor clam.

The common razor clam is known as *Ensis directus,* often just as the *Ensis,* and grows to ten inches long. Sometimes you see this variety sticking halfway up out of mud flats. If so, try to get them. Before grabbing, you might even wish to watch one as it burrows, moving from a horizontal to a vertical position with wonderful grace and seeming mystery. I find them sweet and delicious, and in China they are eaten in huge quantities; unfortunately for me, they are less abundant on Shelter Island than they were ten or fifteen years ago.

Patience and concentration will lead to success in digging steamers, and even if you gather relatively few clams on an outing, you will have had a good time. To walk along the beach at low tide, observing the kaleidoscope of the ocean's rich life, is an invitation to reflect on your life in a quiet and uncluttered way. Clamming connects us to our innate desire to live off the land, and to explore a state of harmony in nature that few other activities reveal so vividly. All this, and a good meal too—can anyone ask for more?

3.
Hardshell Clams

If the steamer is known for its feisty defiance and a fast getaway, the quahog (*Venus mercenaria* is the northern one), sometimes called the Round Clam or simply the Hard-Shelled Clam, is known for its deceptive resilience. Because it has very short siphons, and thus sits right beneath the surface of muddy and sandy estuary and bay bottoms, you would think that it would be very easy to dig up. In fact, however, like the steamer, the quahog instinctively moves to escape our predation. Although much easier to dig than the steamer, it is still no pushover. A really large quahog can challenge the strongest forearm on the other end of the rake.

The common hard-shelled clam or quahog (its widely used Indian name, pronounced quō-hog, has several different spellings) resides primarily in either muddy bottoms of shallow bays, flats, and estuaries or in the somewhat sandier bay bottoms of deeper water. The quahog burrows and moves around. Unlike the "gaping" steamer, however, it can remain firmly closed for long periods of time, and thus it can stay fresher longer, which is why hard-shelled clams and oysters—which can also completely seal up for long periods of time—are so viable for growing and harvesting commercially (because there is plenty of "closed" time in which they can be shipped to markets and restaurants).

The two equal and symmetrical valves of the hard-shelled clam are held together by a strong, rubbery ligament at the hinge. This is the partly visible dark brown raised ridge at the thickest (and therefore oldest) part of the clam. The quahog's strong foot allows it to move around easily and to travel considerable distances. There are many hybrids of the quahog, and the Black Clam is a popular one, but most of these do not have the bright purple stain inside the shell, the attractive part used by the Indians as wampum.

The quahog is a dense, thick clam. If you hold the inside body of a quahog in one hand, and its removed valves in the other, you will feel dramatically that most of the quahog's heavy weight is in the shell—which is why they are ground up and used in road construction. (Clam and oyster shells are also used to make a "shell grit," which is fed to poultry commercially, and the calcium tablets you take typically come from ground oyster shells.) This heaviness keys us in to the best way to discover a quahog.

The first time I went to dig quahogs, I kept asking, "How do I know when I find one?" In some ways it is easier to *show* someone the answer than to tell them, but let me try. As with the steamer, the quahog's *habitat, locomotion,* and *style of eating* give us our first directions for how to catch it. Because it is heavy, large, and unable to move quickly, and because it has a hatchet-shaped foot with which it digs into the sand, occupying a sessile or stationary role most of the time, the quahog is easily detected with your rake. This is the key to knowing when you have found one: If you learn from the beginning to clam by first pushing the rake lightly *away* from your body, you will discover that most other objects your rake hits will roll away, bump out of your path; this includes stones, most whelks and conches, old shells, crabs, and virtually everything except for the clam whose foot anchors it in place. When your rake hits a quahog, alarming it instantly, its foot pulls it more tightly into a fixed position. Therefore, *when you feel your rake hit something hard, and it does not move, especially after you have run the rake back and forth over it a few times, the odds are that you have found a quahog.*

Clam rake.

If you lift your rake slightly off the bottom, then push it away from you again lightly, you will generally knock a little more sand or mud off the top of the hard clam. In this way you will begin to "feel" more of the clam's surface as it is exposed; the teeth of your rake will be sending a tremor up your arms for a split second longer. Although the quahog is very strong, its body shape makes it impossible for it to retreat as rapidly as the steamer.

Once you have found a quahog with your rake, move your rake basket directly behind the clam and dig down. In a matter of seconds you will loosen it. Then pull the rake toward you and, as you bring the basket to the surface, turn the handle so you will be "scooping" it right side up. This sequence of brushing over the top a few times, digging from behind, and scooping works very efficiently. After you gain more experience, you will be able to feel all the objects at the bottom as if you were actually touching them with your hands. As a right-hander (reverse if necessary), I like to cup my right hand over the end of the rake handle when I find a clam, and push it away while pulling the lower part of the rake handle toward me with my left hand. This motion, very much the same as paddling a canoe, amounts to prying the quahog loose from the bottom and sweeping it toward you. Your rake basket is behind the clam

Digging a quahog.

and thus your canoe-paddle motion uses leverage to strengthen the pressure being exerted behind it.

As you pull your rake up, you will learn quickly to tell by the weight not only whether you have a lot of glunk and seaweed but whether you also have a quahog or two. If you do bring up clams and seaweed together, this is not a problem. Be careful to pull the seaweed and any other extraneous material out of the basket carefully. You never know when there might be a sharp piece of broken shell or metal.

When you are digging quahogs you have a fuller kind of physical encounter with the sea than when you dig steamers. Sometimes you are out in the water anywhere from your knees up to your chest, and thus your "universe" is inherently more complex and challenging than the edge of the shoreline. While you usually go for quahogs at low tide, there is nothing to prevent you from going for several hours on either side of low tide. I often go for quahogs when the tide is partly risen, often for an hour or more beyond low tide, especially if it's very hot and I *want* to be more fully immersed in the water. If there are green-eyed flies around, the more of you in the water, the better, for it is easier to dunk down to avoid them.

The typical quahog is between four and five inches long and from one to three inches thick. A good, solid big one, ideal for chowder, will get even larger, and six to twelve of them will make a chowder. When you go for quahogs you may well find many of different sizes, ranging down to the size you want to eat raw on the half shell.

Before we get too far into the art of digging quahogs, let us be sure you know how to begin. First, you should probably wear old sneakers, as you will be in water where either the bottom is unclear or will be made unclear by your digging. For millions of years, people have "treaded" for clams with their bare feet, but I recommend this only faintheartedly, as civilization has brought more dangerous objects into the water. You need a strong, long-handled clam rake in good condition. Examine it carefully before you set out. After enough use, a clam rake rusts, particularly where the basket is attached to the stem of the handle. If this spot gets too rusty, it will break off when you are in the middle of clamming and blacksmiths with forges are scarce (although there is a good one in Greenport). You really want to have a rake that will do the job.

You need to decide, before you start, how you are going to keep the quahogs as you dig them, and how you are going to get them home. Here are some alternatives. I like to use an old-fashioned clam basket with two wooden sides and two large-hole heavy-duty screen sides and a screen bottom with several reinforcing slats of wood suspended from an arched bentwood handle. I tie it around my waist or to the waist-string of my bathing trunks. This kind of basket floats as you begin, and when you have about eight or nine good-sized quahogs, it sinks to the bottom, at which time I keep it beneath my feet, and continue to place carefully into it each quahog as I dig it up. When the basket is full, I stop. In most communities the individual clammer is allowed to take a peck of clams a day, which is plenty.

Often I use a metal clam basket, available in most hardware and marine stores in coastal towns. I tie it to my waist and place it beneath my feet on the bottom. When I begin, I usually put a large rock in it to keep it standing straight so that any current will not tip it over before I have enough clams in it to keep it settled squarely on the bottom.

Another good way to keep your quahogs as you dig them up is to take an inner tube with you and tie either a wooden or a metal basket in the middle of

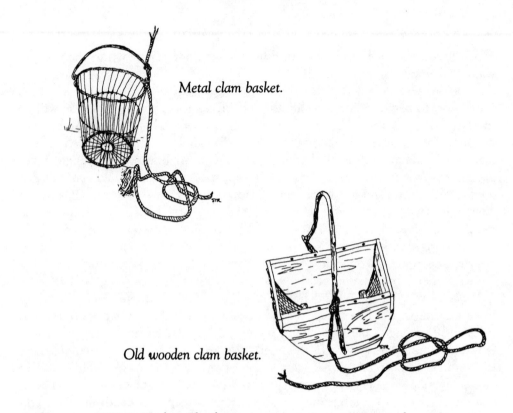

Metal clam basket.

Old wooden clam basket.

it. You can tie it into the tube however you want, sometimes by tying a rope around the tube and then the basket to the rope. The basket can be fully sunk or partly up. Then a rope from the tube should be tied around your waist or chest. The basket can sit in a kind of loose rope cradle, or even be wedged into the tube if the top of the basket is of larger diameter than its bottom, as with the standard metal clam basket. The tube will float to your side as you dig for quahogs, keeping the quahogs in water in the basket and not burdening you with any weight. The tube can also come in handy as a life-protection device if you run into any trouble or get stuck in mud on an incoming tide. In all these ways you are keeping the quahogs in an ideally clean environment, and each enables you to get them back ashore fairly easily since their weight will not be felt below the water. You can also take a large plastic pail which you sink with a rock and place between your feet until the clams make it secure against the water's movements. No matter which device you use, when you are back on shore the clams will represent dead weight and you will need to carry them.

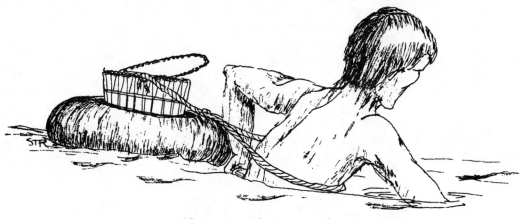

Clamming with an innertube.

There are different ways to "work" the bottom of a bay for quahogs. I find the very best movement is in a circular pattern. I work the bottom by pushing my rake back and forth (starting always with an away motion), while slowly turning my entire body to the left (go right if you are left-handed) a full 360 degrees. Assuming I am pushing the rake five or six feet away from me as I turn, I can cover a bottom area of over 140 square feet very quickly.

Digging quahogs has more mystery than digging steamers. When you gather steamers you are actually "mining" a small area of the beach, but when you go for quahogs you typically cover a much larger area, and the rake becomes eye as well as hand. Usually you can't see the bottom clearly, as you can when digging steamers, and you simply venture out to new parts of the bay.

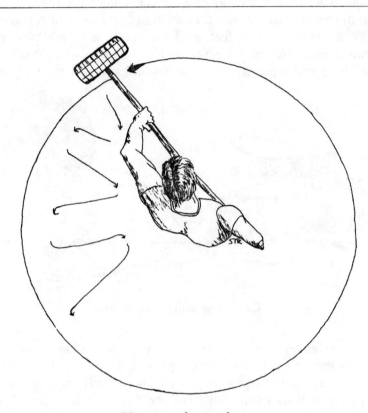

How to gather quahogs.

The waters surrounding Shelter Island have many ancient clam bars, only some of which have been discovered.

Unlike the brittle, soft shells of the steamer, the quahog has such a thick and powerful shell that you tend to hold it in your hand with awe. There is no way you can pry it open. The younger quahogs tend to have more noticeable ridges in concentric circles on the outside of the shells. Their basic color is gray, but they more typically appear partly or quite completely stained either black or brown from the surrounding mud. When you bring one out of your rake basket, always rub off all the excess mud and sand.

While generally you will be digging quahogs in bays that are shallow, they can live happily in depths of up to sixty feet. They tend to like a slightly higher salinity than steamers, and in fact even taste a bit saltier when they are cooked, partly because they are adding a good amount of retained sea water to the pot as you cook them open.

When digging quahogs you often encounter other creatures that ought to be anticipated. This also argues for the strategy of first pushing the rake away from you. Often in the same area in which you are looking for quahogs there will be a horseshoe crab *(Limulus polyphemus)*, for example, a disconcerting creature to pull close to you which will generally bang into your legs and give you a start. The horseshoe crab, incidentally, will not harm you, and it also enjoys eating clams, which it grinds with its tough foot bottoms.

The Channeled Whelk *(Busycon canaliculatum)* is another avid predator of bivalves and competes aggressively with you for quahogs. If you are clamming off a boat, standing in the water and dropping the quahogs from your rake over the stern into a basket in the boat, you should do the same when you catch whelks and conches. Some shellfish ordinances even require you to do so, as opposed to leaving these clam predators in the water. Some people, inciden-

Channeled whelk.

tally, enjoy boiling whelks, removing the meat, pounding it until it softens (it's very hard at first), and thinly slicing it and serving it with sauces (scungilli).

You also may encounter starfish. Along the Atlantic coast the most common is the Northern Sea Star *(Asterias vulgaris)*. This is also a menace to clams, and it is not uncommon to find one completely wrapped around a clam that you find partly out on the bottom. Starfish eat bivalves by wrapping themselves tightly around them and, through their tiny mouths, they send their stomachs inside the clamshell and envelop the entire body of the clam and proceed to digest it. The suction power is incredible. In addition to starfish, horseshoe crabs, whelks, and conches, you are also apt to find sea squirts or tunicates, little puffed up bloblike creatures anywhere between one and three inches in diameter. They often end up impaled on the end of your rake tongs, in which case you simply slide them off and let them drop back into the water. Encountering these and other creatures is all part of the excitement and education of clamming.

As when digging steamers, you want to maximize your efficiency when you are digging quahogs. And with quahogs, it is easier. If you have found a quahog and are now coming from behind it and dislodging it, and you hit *another* hard object that *also* doesn't move, you are probably hitting the top of another quahog. Use your rake to loosen this one as well as the first *before* you pull up the rake. If you neglect the second one while you are after the first, already loosened one, you may miss it. Unlike the steamer, the quahog can't pull down rapidly. The loosened quahog will be very available for enough time so that you can safely make a start on the second or others. Then bring them all to the surface together. The "prying" method works very well because once the first quahog is popped loose, it is *all the way loose,* which gives you time to get another, or several, loose and then gather them all up. Clams are gregarious and like to be together. In your enthusiasm for number one or even two, you don't want to miss a chance at also getting numbers three and four.

If quahogs are not turning up in an area that generally is known to have some, be sure that you are using your rake directly on the bottom. If you feel large ups and downs of the bottom itself, you may be clamming in an area that has been dug heavily. When a quahog has been dug out of the bottom, it leaves a good-sized hole which takes quite a while to smooth out. Try moving slowly, taking baby steps. If the terrain beneath your feet goes up and down, you are clearly working over an area too recently dug by others. Keep moving slowly around and there is often a good chance that you will find a flat-bottomed area, a section of bottom *within* a general area that has been heavily dug. I did this the other day in West Neck Harbor and proceeded to find about twenty in one "circle" pass.

If you feel a solid "bang" on your rake tongs, the likely sign of a quahog, but then *don't* find it as you put your rake back over it and move on to another pass, go back and keep looking for the other one. It's very easy, especially at first, to lose confidence and convince yourself that maybe you just had hit a rock or that you were not going back to the right spot. Always keep looking. Here's the point to remember: There *has* to be an explanation, a cause, for the thudding sensation you had, and you should not feel satisfied until you either dig up a quahog or find whatever it is that caused the sensation in the first place. This is particularly important to watch for when you are digging one clam and your tongs alert you to other "bumps" nearby. Quahogs can and do pile on top of one another. An area can be thick with quahogs, particularly if you stumble into a bed for the first time. So, again, the main thing is to *keep working over the area until you account for every bump.* This is quahog-gathering at its very best.

When you do find that the explanation for a bump is a rock or a whelk, flip it out of your rake and toss it back into the area you have just come from; there is no point in finding "it" again. Some clammers like to work the bottom in a direct forward path, rather than in the circular style, and this of course makes it particularly easy to leave a trail of discarded objects behind you.

There are different kinds of clam beds and bottom conditions and they need to be approached a bit differently, although the basic tools and body movements are the same. Soft sandy bottoms of the deeper bays are ideal because the clams are easier to dislodge. You can walk more comfortably on a clear, relatively flat bottom, and you can sometimes see it clearly, depending on wind and water movements. In contrast to these flat, smooth bottoms are the more jagged bottoms where one comes upon accumulated rough, coarser piles of debris, clam beds that are whole systems of life, supporting numerous crabs and creatures in a state of mutual interdependency. These beds have a denser and more challenging character and you may well have to dig your rake tongs into the sand farther, exerting yourself more.

When you are on a sandy bottom, you can walk around fairly sure that the bottom is firm and will not give way on you. On the other hand, you can sink suddenly and unexpectedly when exploring a soft or seemingly coarse bottom, particularly because in the latter there tend to be ridges immediately followed by drops into channels of deeper water, often of several feet. You can sink deep into mud bottom flats, and when exploring these it is imperative to walk very slowly, letting your weight fully settle on one foot, so you know how deep it is sinking in, before bringing the other foot forward. This may seem tedious, and you are walking very slowly, but you are reducing the risk of having one foot go plunging too deeply. When that happens, the surprise stimulates you to move hard and fast, usually sinking you in even deeper. You should turn your body carefully, and avoid screwing yourself into the bottom like a corkscrew. Captain Frank Beckwith tells the story of how one day, around the turn of the century, a man went out clamming at low tide in Shelter Island's Congdon Creek. The hours went by and the man didn't return. He was found dead, right where he was clamming, stuck in the mud. The tide had come in over his head.

So you have to be careful with each step when you explore unfamiliar areas. Incidentally, if at any time in your life you are in a bed of quicksand, which is highly unlikely, don't try to "walk" out of it. Instead, throw yourself on top of it spread-eagled and work your way out. By distributing your body weight across a larger surface, you may avoid being sucked under.

All clammers make mistakes, and you will too. Some years ago, for example, I felt what I thought was a quahog in my clam rake but I just could not seem to dig it out. Finally, in desperation, I reached down with my hand and grabbed it with all my strength. The pain was so intense that I screamed as I came up with a large broken conch shell, the edge of which had worn very thin. I walked to shore, went to the first house I could find where, fortunately, there was someone to drive me to the hospital where I had to have stitches to stop the bleeding. I have never again used my hand "blindly" like that when digging quahogs. For similar reasons, *don't pull the rake basket too close to your feet.* Instead, move back and keep pulling the rake after you. If your tongs slip off the clam, they may strike your leg.

Since digging quahogs is physically more demanding than digging steamers (one gets clammer's elbow the same as tennis elbow), think about ways to build some relaxing steps into the process. To begin with, you do not need to grip the rake with all your strength in both hands when you are searching for quahogs. If you are right-handed, place your right hand firmly at the end of the handle and your left hand loosely around the middle to upper portion. With your right arm, in a slow-motion piston movement, push the rake back and forth over the bottom. When you find a clam, tighten your left hand grip and put more strength into the process, ideally a "prying" out of the clam. Also, when you turn your body, which will be to the left if you are right-handed, let your feet and legs glide rather than making deliberate moves—as if you were almost swimming for a few seconds. When you bring up a quahog, rub it clean in the water and place it in the basket, rather than lifting the basket up to you. If you are clamming in deeper water, you may have to stick your head under water to reach the basket on the bottom. Go ahead and "take the plunge," because if you simply drop the clam over the basket, there is no guarantee that it will go straight down to it.

Occasionally you will feel a bumpy ridge rather than a single object. This can be a very good sign. What I think of as a "cobblestone-road feeling" is often a large bunch of quahogs. Run your rake back and forth over the length of the ridge, and if nothing is moving, start digging down behind the farthest edge. Keep working the rake basket toward you, loosening the quahogs consecutively. On a "cobblestone" bed like this, you can bring up three or four at a time. If you feel from your feet that there are quahogs directly beneath you, get the ones that are farthest away first, then walk backward five feet and begin raking over the area where you were standing.

One important general rule applies to quahogs as well as to steamers. Try to go where others have not been digging. Remember, if the bottom suddenly becomes pockmarked or filled with "minicraters," keep walking and find a flatter spot. The "going-farther" mind-set should encourage you to go out into deeper water, unless it is cold and you are wearing waders rather than a swimming suit. In good weather, all you have to be able to do is breathe and get your rake to the bottom.

I recently arrived at a clamming spot where I have dug quahogs on and off for twenty years. Another clammer there complained that he was finding very few, and that he had recently seen some twenty people digging in this area. Very quickly I knew he was telling the truth (I never assume the truth, however, since I know people will lie about anything, including the tide, to discourage you from clamming in "their" spot), because I could feel that the bottom had been dug. So, I walked out up to my neck—it was dead low tide—knowing that I was getting virtually as far as anyone could, and guessing that not many would bother to go out that far. I managed to get three dozen in good time.

When you have had good luck at finding quahogs, try with your mind's eye to draw a picture or map by looking at all the land identification you can, mentally forming *intersecting* lines. You can be out in the bay and line up on a tree, only to realize later that it looked the same for several hundred yards parallel to the shore. Check all directions for markers of any kind: buoys, houses, trees, rocks, and so forth. Also, as you walk back to shore, stop every so often and check out areas. This gives you a possible head start on your next outing, when you might not have as much time. It's fun to know where there are clams still to be dug, to have them, like "clams" in the vernacular, in the bank.

The clam rake needs to be used almost like a dancing partner, not just as an instrument. It is extremely versatile. Just as there are now large spiderlike machines that use their robot arms as they move around on the ocean floor and pick things up, so the clam rake can be made to function like a third arm and "hand"—which is the essence of its design. For example, I use the rake as a guide and "clearance" stick, something like the blind person's cane. When I venture into new waters to search for quahogs, I often stop and put the rake well in front of me and push against the bottom to see how soft it is. More than once this has kept me from sinking suddenly when out on the flats. I also use the rake to test for the amount of seaweed present. I have caught crabs with it by slamming it down on top of a protruding blue claw. Sometimes when startled by something hitting my leg (like a fish or eel), I have even flipped myself up off the ground with it like a pole vaulter.

The clam rake can be used as a good long arm to get oysters off rocks on the bottom or scallops off the back of a boat (see chapter 4). I've even tried to come down on an eel with my rake, but so far unsuccessfully.

Let's switch location. Along many shores, and especially where tributaries open into larger areas of water, you will often be able to find hard-shelled clams sitting suspended in silt that covers the bottom. This grayish-brown murky substance teems with microscopic life and is thus a good place in which hard-shelled clams with their short siphons can suspend themselves and feed. Getting them out of it is relatively easy, certainly easier than prying them from the bottom in deep water, though that is still my preference.

By pushing your rake back and forth in the thick silty mixture you will discover few hard objects of clam size, and very few whelks or conches. When you hit something big and hard, it is usually a clam. There is no reason for a rock to be up off the ground, but a clam has a reason for being there. Once you strike the hard object—and again, after awhile you'll always be able to "feel" that it's a clam—usually with the back of your rake in the first instance, maneuver your rake to get under it and scoop it out. As you pull the rake up, jump the handle up and down in the water, thereby diluting the mud and rinsing it out of the rake. When you can, use your hand to reach into the remaining mud carefully and pull the clam out. Rinse it fully and put it with your others.

If you are looking for hard-shelled clams in such locations, including flats, creeks, estuaries, and edges of the shore near tributaries and channels, you will often find a mix of sizes from small to large, though the very largest are almost always found farther out in the deeper water. I try to check out all the parts of the creek, the edges, the middle, even up onto grasses on shore, where oysters may be beginning a colony. If you are bent on gathering cherrystones and you come upon a large quahog, keep it and see if you have more. There's no point in taking home two or three large ones to cook open, but once you're over a half-dozen, it's worth it. If at the end of your outing you have only one or two of the huge size, just toss them back (unless of course, like me, you plan to be going out the next day for larger ones anyway).

When you see people digging quahogs out in the bays, standing in water up to their chests, remember that there may be some quahogs very close to shore that people walk right by. This is the opposite advice of going as far out as you can—try exploring close to land as well. Hard-shelled clams will not be abundant close to shore, but few people bother to look there and you may be the one to get those there are. Even if the bottom is hard and sandy, as is likely, try making three or four "circle" passes. Unlike steamers, quahogs turn up in a variety of places and depths, and most of them grow to a good size in five or six years—except the deep-sea clam *Tindaria callistiformis* of the North Atlantic, which takes over a hundred years to reach its size of eight millimeters, or .31 inches, the slowest grower in the animal kingdom!

If you set out to dig quahogs in tidal flats of shallow water, be sure to approach the large open area carefully. Often you will be following a narrow creek part of the way, the route that brings the ocean into the more expansive flatland with its softer bottoms. This route can vary enormously in bottom composition, and thus it is very important to walk along the edges carefully, especially when you are on unfamiliar clamming ground. Once out on the flats you are apt to find some soft areas. If you sink in too deep, back up very slowly. Remember, if you panic, you will only sink in deeper.

Be sure to keep an eye out for razor clams along the shore edges. Since razor clams are often found in the same area as hard-shelled clams, you may spot some sticking halfway up. Dig down hard under them quickly.

Yesterday I went for quahogs, and although I'm not writing a diary, it was a fairly typical hot August day, and summarizing it may be helpful. Low tide was scheduled for 2 P.M. I looped my plastic-encased shellfishing permit around my neck, put on some old sneakers and a bathing suit, and headed for the south shore of the island. I arrived at 1 P.M. so I would be able to dig first in areas where I suspected others had been digging recently, but then would also be able to go out as far as possible into the West Neck Bay when the tide was fully receded. I figured I could get in a good forty minutes in the most distant, reachable spot, where the clams would be their densest.

Before walking the full length of the shoreline, I wandered out into the nearer water to look for a clam bar I had discovered about ten years ago and haven't found since. It must be like Atlantis—I still haven't found it.

I walked out up to my waist and started digging. They came slowly at first, one every so often, sometimes two in each circle pass. I walked closer to a section I had avoided just a few days earlier, not wanting to clam too close to a man who had arrived ahead of me. My rake brought up a young, light-tan horseshoe crab. When I put it back in the water it swam around on its back, comical as a scallop in its jerky movements. Then it almost playfully came toward me. I took the rake, scooped it up, and tossed it farther away. Once again it came toward me. I finally realized that it was trying to get back to the same spot where I had found it, so I left it alone, and sure enough, after a few more minutes, it disappeared from beside me back to the bottom. Horseshoe crabs have been around since prehistoric times and are the subject of a great deal of research, including their potential uses in medicine. If you find a bunch of tiny green eggs in the sand in the spring when you are digging for steamers, leave them alone: they are horseshoe-crab eggs and should not be disturbed.

Scientists need them for specimens, particularly for research into their incredibly successful longevity as a species. Like the cockroach and the shark, the horseshoe crab has a good thing going and has not changed significantly in millions of years.

The bottom was, as usual, very sandy, with the usual signs of diversity evident in the tongs of my rake—small conch shells, sea grasses, empty jingle shells, and an occasional baby scallop. At one point I brought up a colorful duo of a rock crab and a large whelk. The crab clattered and clawed in my rake basket until I turned it over and watched it disappear.

As the tide moved out, I followed it and was able to get a good third of the way across the bay. A solitary tern dove straight into the water for a shiner a few feet away, reminding me once again of their great beauty and accuracy.

I had tied the metal clam basket rope to the string of my bathing suit. (Once I went without a rope tied to a plastic pail, and lost my bearings at one point, and never recovered the pail.) I placed my basket on the bottom between my feet. I began digging and quickly found several quahogs together. Encouraged, I reraked the same area and found more. I moved slowly in a circle and kept picking them up. I have consistently found that when you are not finding many, you should run your rake lightly and quickly in large push-and-pull motions, but when you are doing well, you should keep raking very hard and in a narrower range. Once you are finding them, you should be sure to cover every inch of the bottom in that spot. My basket began to fill up.

As I moved farther out I began to find fewer in clusters but managed to keep finding individual clams. After an hour or so, I knew this would be one of my better days of the summer. I headed for the shore, then walked in the water parallel to the shore along the beach, letting the water support the weight of the clams in my basket.

A woman carrying a reference book approached me as I stepped onto the beach and asked enthusiastically about the clams I had dug. I explained that they were northern quahogs. To my good fortune, she turned out to be a marine biologist from British Columbia, which gave me an opportunity to learn more about the gooeyduck clams, the gigantic gaping soft-shelled clams that are abundant in the Pacific Northwest. She said she caught them often and was apt to either boil or bake *one* for dinner. I then proceeded to teach her son how to dig quahogs and he learned very quickly, as anyone can. Later in the day I gave some of my quahogs to Libby Heineman, one of Shelter Island's best clam chefs who has generously given me several of her outstanding recipes (see chapter 5).

Sighting a black skimmer.

Gathering quahogs is a particularly quiet activity because you are out in the water and virtually away from any sound. Geese sometimes fly low over your head, as do gulls, terns, and cormorants. Occasionally a black skimmer goes whizzing by, less than a foot above the water, as it begins to hunt for the small fish driven out by the receding tide from the estuary grasses into the deeper water.

As you walk back, you typically follow silence with beauty by observing seaweed, limpet shell clusters, rolling stones at the water's edge, all catching the afternoon sun and flickering it to you sporadically. Back home I was at the typewriter watching some fledgling mockingbirds in our dogwood tree, but my thoughts were of the bay.

As I gathered quahogs I tried, on this occasion, to make a short mental list of a few further tips to share. If you are having trouble at first when you are using the clam rake, ask someone to show you how to hold it. It's comparable to asking someone to show you how to swing a golf club. If a crab clings to your rake when you bring it up, first try to shake it loose. If it hangs on, you can either shake it harder or grab it (at least a rock crab) from behind the carapace where it can't reach you with its claws (same for a blue claw, which you should grab by the flipper behind the carapace). Remember to carry the clams back in the water as long as you possibly can. Remember, too, that success breeds success. Keep reworking vigorously an area that has begun to yield well. Also, if you need to cross deeper water in order to come back "up" to a shallower bay bottom, go toward shore and walk around the channel area. Don't try to swim with your basket, especially if it is tied to you. If it is a short distance, you might be all right, but if the channel of deeper water you are crossing turns out to be wider than you expected, you are taking a great risk. Never underestimate the pull of the tide. It can make swimming much harder than usual, and when you add to this the notion of trying to tread water and swim simultaneously in water over your head, you can get tired very quickly.

Sometimes you will want to go in a boat to an area where you can dig quahogs. In Coecles Harbor, for example, on Shelter Island, a boat gets you into good areas of the bay's bottom that you could not easily walk to from any point on land. The important thing to remember about clamming next to your boat, when you reach the area you want to try, is what the tide is doing. If, for example, you begin clamming before low tide and through it, when the tide is rising, the boat will be rising too, and you have to be sure the boat is well anchored. A friend of mine was once clamming next to his boat when the bay constable appeared and asked to see his license. The constable tied his boat alongside my friend's and soon the two boats began to drift on the single anchor out into deeper water—as the tide was rising. Eventually they were able to get back, but it was a harrowing experience.

·   ·   ·

Clamming is more than something I do. It is something I experience. Standing still, alone at the edge of the water on a long stretch of deserted beach, or walking slowly through an inland saltwater marsh at low tide, I feel very much at peace with an unchanging part of the world. I find it easy to center myself in this world that is characterized by natural bouquets of sea lavender, by sea grasses quivering in the breeze, by a great blue heron that, startled by my intrusion, rises suddenly out of the grass and lumbers across the water to a farther marsh, by a trio of loons that disappear under water.

Searching out and digging quahogs brings me into moments of natural stillness, into a sense of respectful partnership with nature. I deeply enjoy doing something I know that others have done for generations before me and that people will continue to do for centuries into the future. I look down the beach a last time before I go. Canada geese that departed when I showed up are now returning and settling quietly, reclaiming their place. Plovers and sandpipers have returned to scurry along the water's edge. On an old bulkhead, the sea gulls are back, their heads all turned toward the incoming tide.

4.
Oysters, Mussels, and Scallops

Oysters, mussels, and scallops are an important part of our seafood heritage, and even though we ourselves seem—at least for now—to have moved fully out of the sea onto land, a part of us is still soulfully tied to the sea. In that sense we have a natural affinity for other creatures that seem still to be negotiating their own relationships to the sea, to its complexities and tides. Oysters and mussels form huge colonies that in turn sustain many other marine animals, and scallops keep us guessing because they resist ironclad patterns of habitat and conduct. All three bivalves provide fascinating examples of the impressive adaptations that marine life continuously exhibits. Each also represents an important part of the ocean's food supply, and from the vertical scallop baskets pulled up every two years in Japan to the layers of oyster spat in flat-bottom beds off Long Island, these bivalves are the focus of an enormous amount of cultivation and research.

Oysters have a kind of "good old boy" character. They tend to be unflatteringly large in the bottom, bulky, set in their ways, and tenacious, while at the same time inspiring many good one-liners in literature. As bivalves go, they are uncharacteristically quite *different* from one another. Mussels, in contrast, seem less like character studies. They bunch together like oysters but tend to grow more uniformly in their shape and they seem visually more attractive, their wet blue-black sheen suggesting well-trained military in uniform. If the oyster seems a bit of a curmudgeon and the mussel a shiny recruit, the scallop is a highly improvisational actor whose quickness and nervous movement catch the eye fancifully. Each of these three, in any event, is a wonderful creature with distinctive characteristics that provide us with the chief clues to gathering them successfully.

OYSTERS

Oysters are grown commercially on a very large scale, particularly along the Atlantic coast from Rhode Island to Virginia, off Louisiana, and off Washington State. They are often cultivated vertically, as are scallops, although up until 1923 the spat was typically placed on roofing tiles and shells in flat bottoms. Generally considered the most prolific and most harvested bivalve, the naturally settled oyster is not always easily found by the individual. Long associated with the lustrous pearls that grow naturally inside them, and which for many centuries in Europe could be worn only by royalty, (in Europe before 1720 it was against the law for commoners to wear them), oysters have always been sought out eagerly by divers, especially those of the *Pinctada* and *Pteria* genera. Pearls turn up regularly in Egyptian, Greek, and Roman archeological digs.

Today pearls, like oysters, are grown and harvested commercially, both in this country and in Japan. The oyster secretes a material that has the same bright iridescence as the inside of its shell and, as it builds around a tiny object that irritates it, a pearl is formed. The "assist" pearls are given by being formed around implanted pieces of plastic and shell (instead of natural irritants like sand grains and tiny worms) are a good example of the potential for science to be a worthy handmaiden to nature. In the twelfth century in China people began putting tiny Buddha figures inside mussels and found that a few years later they could remove them with a beautiful mother-of-pearl sheen. It was this process that led Kokichi Mikimoto to take the lead and win enduring fame by inserting "irritants" into oysters. Mikimoto perfected his process around 1908 when he was fifty years old and pursued his interest avidly until he died at age ninety-six, frequently attributing his old age to taking calcium pills daily!

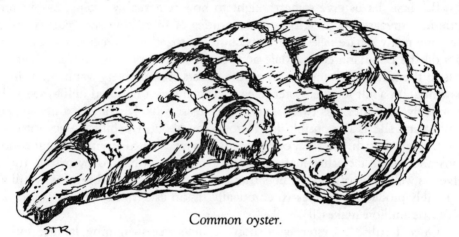

Common oyster.

Most oysters range from four to ten inches and their valves are gray green and rough, often marked with many tiny holes drilled by sponges. Oysters feed heartily and grow relatively fast as the cilia on their gills steadily sweep in water bearing planktonic food at a rate estimated by some scientists to be about twenty-five gallons a day.

The American oyster, also generally known as the Eastern oyster or the common oyster (*Crassostrea virginica*) lives both between the low and high tide lines and in depths of forty feet, usually attached to rocks, shells, and other oysters. This oyster is abundant in waters along the entire Atlantic coast, the

Gulf of Mexico, and the Pacific Coast. Like all oysters, the Eastern oyster comes in various shapes, is often pear-shaped, and becomes sessile or stationary at a very early stage by "cementation" to rocks, other oysters, and hard objects. It then most typically remains attached for the duration of its life, though sometimes strong winds and currents loosen them and you can find them lying in solitude closer to the shore's edges. That it lives both above the low-tide mark and in deeper waters provides the key to harvesting it in a variety of ways, two of which I will describe shortly.

But first, let us give some thought to how remarkably prolific oysters are. Extremely gregarious, they form communities of incredible size. For example, there are many square *miles* of oysters clustered together on reefs outside certain bays off the Louisiana coast. Male and female oysters typically release their sex cells in the spring and summer when the waters are relatively warm. In a single spawning, an adult female oyster releases as many as a hundred million eggs. If, as is likely, she does this twice a year, and if, as is likely, she has a life span of eight years, she is responsible for introducing about 1.6 billion eggs into the water. Even though less than one percent survive, due to environmental conditions and to the fact that many are unwittingly cannibalized by oysters themselves as well as by other creatures that thrive on planktonic life, this is still an incredibly productive species (theoretically, as an aside, only one egg of a codfish's one million makes it).

Once fertilized, oyster eggs soon become free-swimming larvae, microscopic organisms first called trochophores, about 1/40th of an inch in size, then veliger larvae, top-shaped with a tuft of cilia. Each initially looks like a miniature clam. After a while, the tiny oyster drops to the bottom and for a short time goes exploring with its foot. It then secretes a kind of glue or cement and attaches itself permanently, usually to rocks or to other oysters. Once attached, it is called a "spat," and begins its rapid growth. Oysters form attached groups or clusters known as "hands" of oysters, and thus you typically find bunches of them together. They are often covered with other creatures, particularly mussels and barnacles. You need not be concerned about what you find on the outside of the oyster, as you will only be eating the inside. Boring sponges, starfish, oyster drills, and other creatures all attack the oyster regularly and represent your greatest competition in getting enough oysters to serve that Oysters Rockefeller you are contemplating as you stand there in the marsh.

The oyster's valves, like those of the hard-shelled clam, are hinged together by a strong elastic ligament. They open and close in the same way as those of the scallop, a movement controlled by a strong single adductor muscle (the clam, remember, has both anterior and posterior muscles). Unlike the clam, the oyster is very narrow at the hinge, with a long, curved "umbo". Its bumps, grooves, and hard waviness make it an ideal "home" for many other creatures, which is why oyster beds are teeming with life of all kinds. When you pull an oyster out of the water, you typically are bringing many other creatures along with it, though most will not easily be seen.

I like to gather oysters as an extension of clamming, and as they are harder to find, I don't gather nearly so many. Essentially I proceed in two ways, depending on the habitat.

On some parts of the coast the Eastern oyster lives happily above the tide line. It can be seen in clusters or alone sticking up at the edge of the shore where it is often attached to the bottoms of grasses, to other oysters, or to dead shells. Where there are a lot of them, these oysters can appear to be almost lying flat, though most often they are sticking straight up with their sharp edges protruding. If I am digging cherrystones or hunting for steamers, I always check the edges of the shore for oysters. You need to look very carefully to spot the first one, especially because they blend in with the typical colors surrounding them, but when you do, the odds are that you will find at least several more and sometimes a good bunch. While oysters are prolific in their reproduction cycles and in commercial underwater harvesting, they can be fairly difficult to find in large numbers in the creeks and marshes.

Sometimes after a storm or rough seas, bunches of oysters will be driven toward shore and can be found simply lying around in the intertidal water where you can simply pick them up by hand. This means removing them from whatever they are attached to. I always keep a clam rake with me. If an oyster is attached to a rock, for example, you can hold the rock in your hand and bang the oyster off by hitting it against the rake basket. In this way you don't cut your hands, and the oyster, when free, drops into the basket rather than into the water, which your tromping around may have muddied and stirred up, thus making it difficult to retrieve an oyster that drops to the bottom. If you find a group of oysters attached to one another, as is common, you can keep them that way until you get home. If you plan to cook them until they open, you will never need to separate them, so why bother? If you are going to shuck them, it is better to do so when you can hold them with a glove, potholder, or kitchen towel. Oysters are ragged and sharp and you must be very careful not to handle them roughly.

The two tricky things about gathering oysters by hand are to be careful not to cut yourself and not to sink into mire. If you see oysters in large numbers on the edge of a shore across the creek from where you are, don't simply proceed to hurry across toward them. They may be abundant because they are inaccessible; there may be deep mud between you and that opposite shore.

When you see oysters sticking up, be sure to look for them under water in the same area. Also, try walking up onto the matted-down grasses, for between the flattened reeds you often will see through to a layer of oysters. Always be on the lookout for the little white splatches of oyster spat, informing you that oysters are in the area. Be sure to know when it is permissible to take oysters and what size they need to be to keep. It takes about five hundred to seven hundred "seed oysters" of an inch in length to cover one acre, and some of them escape from where they are put down and make their way to other areas. This means that solitary oysters can turn up almost anywhere they find a spot to which they can cement themselves. I have found oysters in virtually every kind of marsh, creek, and bay habitat on Shelter Island, and I'm sure they exist, if perhaps less abundantly, in all five of the island's harbors.

The other way for you to gather oysters becomes operative when they are well under water, usually attached to rocks or to one another in anywhere from a few feet to five or more feet (at the far greater depths, you are out of luck). The first thing to do is to locate them, generally by wading into waters off the rocky points of beaches, or by exploring the various bay bottom areas by boat. If you find a bunch on rocks, you can generally get them successfully with either an oyster rake (very much like a garden rake but with curled tongs) or with a clam rake, which, along with my hands, is what I always use. When you bring your rake down on top of the oysters and rocks, then maneuver them up in the basket, you are bringing up a relatively large weight.

On a clear day when the water is still and the sky not so bright as to create reflection, I walk along rocky points keeping whatever shade my body casts directly in front of me to make it easier to see through the water to the bottom. With some experience, you develop an eye for detecting the oysters on the bottom. They look almost like pieces of old mortar or cement. If the water is not too cold, you can reach down and, with almost no pressure at all, lightly touch what you see to confirm the feel of an oyster. Once assured, I use my rake to lift it off the bottom. If you are very careful, you can pick them up with your hands. Hold them lightly so you don't cut yourself. And don't make the mistake I did recently of leaving your clam rake nearby with the teeth facing up. I slipped on the rocks and came down with a hand on one tong, resulting in a puncture. As a rule, I keep the oysters in a metal clam basket, though you can simply place them over the stern of a boat.

Make no mistake about it: There are not tons of natural growth oysters available, but this makes hunting for them that much more fun and challenging. I tend to have the most luck where the ends of the shores meet with large bodies of water and where, additionally, there are rocks on the bottom before you come to the deeper sand and mud. When I do find oysters, they tend to be a good size, significantly larger than the legal minimum of three inches. Also, you don't need to find as many oysters as clams to have a feast. If you are going to serve them on the shell, four or five for each person will suffice, especially if they are large or are going to be "expanded" with spinach, as in Oysters Rockefeller.

Because the oyster season is often short, from September to April, you need to do most of your oystering in the colder months. Oysters typically spawn in May and the summer months. I tend to find my best bunches of good-sized oysters in October and November. (You can shuck oysters and freeze them up to a year in a zip-lock bag). If you are going to be walking around in cold waters, wear a pair of full-size waders, not just hip boots; the odds are you will want to go into the water as far as you possibly can (and if it is cold weather, obviously you cannot bend all the way over to test with your fingers). It's great to combine getting some oysters with an outing to gather the larger steamers available during the spring lower tides. Usually you can "stand" the cold water long enough to get the number you need. On an April day, I'll typically dig the steamers during the low-tide period, then pick up some oysters just as the tide is beginning to rise, and finally pick up some mussels on the way home. In this way I get the biggest steamers, gather the oysters while I can still reach them, and pull up the mussels when they are under water. The sequence is ideal.

For oysters that are in deeper water, and which you cannot reach with your rake, you will need to use oyster "tongs," large wooden-handled tools like kitchen tongs. Oysters harvested commercially are typically brought up this way by men using tongs twenty-five feet long. One man wields the tongs while his companion worker "culls," that is, breaks off the undersized oysters from the legal-size ones. It is very hard work, especially because you are trying to leverage something a good distance away and you have to bring the tongs up such a long way from where you are. I personally have never tried this, and for the individual, the required equipment is formidable.

Oysters take three to five years to reach marketable size, despite their rapid initial growth, but I have found plenty up to ten inches. On commercial oyster farms the oysters are moved every few years, kept together in similar sizes, almost as if they were advancing through elementary school. The massive oyster culturing that takes place inevitably releases oysters of different sizes, which are then carried by the tides to distant settings. Oyster culture takes place in many parts of the world, and especially on our West Coast and in certain parts of France, on the muddy flats exposed during low tide. The flats are periodically covered with dead oyster shells for the oysters to fasten to, but again, many just go their own way. Hunting for oysters will always bring you a few surprises, and there is a good chance that they will turn up in surprising places. In any event, getting your own oysters is fun, and while they may not be abundant, naturally grown oysters are nevertheless around, on both coasts, and you should make them an extra part of your clamming outings.

MUSSELS

Mussels, like oysters, have long been one of man's favorite seafoods. They are enjoyed around the world, on both American coasts, and are farmed commercially, perhaps with most famous success in France, where they are a prized delicacy. As discussed in chapter 5, mussels are best understood by reference to their "byssus," the small bundle of protein fibers they secrete to attach themselves into a stationary position. While the oyster (and the barnacle) secretes a kind of glue to cement one of its valves to a rock, shell, or hard object, the mussel uses its wiry filaments—which are sticky when secreted but harden in a few minutes—to "tie" itself to something firmly set in place.

Mussels have their own style of locomotion and migration. Like clams and oysters they have a great deal of freedom to settle where they want and to attach themselves as they see fit. All mussels, whether of the gigantic size found in the Arctic currents off British Columbia or of the normal two-to three-and-a-half-inch size typical of the Atlantic coast, attach themselves to reeds, rocks, other hard-shelled creatures, and therefore of course quite abundantly to one another. To do this they send out their byssus threads from the base of their extended foot when they are moving, then send out more bunches of threads to make the attachment permanent. Their ability to cling puts Velcro to shame.

Because of its remarkable byssogenous gland, the mussel is able to move with less effort than by using a foot. It goes where whatever it is attached to goes, and I often find clumps of them attached happily to the tails of large pieces of kelp washed up along the ocean coasts of Rhode Island. Although many mussels stay in the same place, they are distributed universally throughout the world. They grow most often in dense beds that are filled with barnacles, crabs, worms, sponges, and various other creatures.

Blue mussel.

The most popular edible mussel is the Blue Mussel, or *Mytilus edulis*. Found most typically on rocky shorelines, and also frequently clinging happily to the ends of horsetail kelp, the blue mussel's name is well deserved, as its relatively small, pointy oval valves are a striking bluish black. It ranges in size up to four inches and is usually found to be about three inches or a little larger. The blue mussel has two umbos, one on each valve, that give it a lumpy pointed end. Its shape is almost triangular. Though commonly attached to rocks, it is found clinging to wood, to dock and marina pilings, and simply in loose clusters of its own between the high and low tide lines.

Like clams, mussels are the focus throughout the world of research activities. In Norway, mussels are used to monitor polycydic aromatic hydrocarbon levels in treated sewage water—not unlike our use of quahogs, along with sandworms and grass shrimp, to test for PCBs in New York Harbor. Since 1974, in experimental plots in Great Sippewissett Marsh, Massachusetts, researchers have been measuring the ribbed mussel, *Modiolus demissus*, along with fiddler crabs, to run experiments on a sewage sludge fertilizer containing large amounts of heavy metals. The future research uses of the mussel cannot be guessed at, but one thing is certain: the popularity of eating mussels is going to accelerate

Ribbed mussel.

in America. The message is being brought with vigor from Europe, particularly from France and Spain.

In addition to the blue mussel, you will also typically gather the ribbed mussel, which is plentiful on Shelter Island. Sometimes known as bank mussels, ribbed mussels (so named because of the tactile ridges you can feel on their valves) tend to cling to banks of grass and stone at the edge of bays and marshes, and can be found in virtually any sort of saltwater inlets. Although not generally offered in restaurants or sold commercially, they are also edible and in fact have a very delicate flavor. With your eyes closed, you would have a hard time differentiating them from blue mussels. But it is very important to check with either state or local offices overseeing shellfishing regulations before eating ribbed mussels, as they sometimes are in brackish water or exposed so long higher up on the shore that they acquire bacteria. If dug under water in a well-circulating saltwater area, they are usually fine, but again, it is best to check. In his *Long Island Seafood Cook Book,* J. George Frederick discusses both types of mussel in a wonderful chapter entitled, "Give the Long Island Mussel Its Due."

Both the ribbed mussel, with its rough radial ribs, and the very smooth blue mussel can be gathered at low tides and both tend to live between the low and high tide lines. It is always best to dig them under water, but there is nothing wrong with digging them partly exposed. Like the steamer clam, the *Mya,* mussels can live out of water a long time. All mussels attach themselves by their pointed end at the bottom, the enlarged posterior part of their shell (the posterior mantle inside the shell is also enlarged, as the larger of the mussel's two adductor mussels is the posterior one).

Although there are freshwater mussels in many ponds, rivers, and lakes in America, they are used primarily for their shells, from which mother-of-pearl buttons are made, and for pearl cultivation, particularly in the Mississippi. To ascertain whether they are edible, consult with state or local authorities.

The shells of mussels, like those of oysters, are slightly open in order to allow the animal to take in planktonic food in the water washing over them. When you grab a mussel it should close very tightly, which indicates it is alive. If it can't be pried open, you can be sure it is very healthy. Since you generally will be cooking it to open in the same way as steamers, it will be safe eating.

Mussels like to congregate in tightly packed beds or groups and they become increasingly tightly packed as they grow older. Because they are fixed in place, eating and growing, they inevitably force one another out of position, and thus the number of mussels in a spot keeps being reduced as their growth takes place. Since mussels live to ten years, it is obvious that many are "lost" by being loosened from their initial settling place. Some of these mussels will find other places to attach, and some will be eaten.

The large middens, or heaps, of shells, which archeologists continue to explore in locations as far away as Alaska and Spain, well remind us how abundantly early man used his hands to get clams and other shellfish from the sea. Gathering mussels is probably the easiest of all seafood quests. You are looking right at them, they sit in front of you, and you put your hands onto them and grab. What could be simpler? When you grab a mussel, however, be sure to grab only one, using your hand to hold down the object or clump of mussels to which the one you have selected is attached. Give a hard twist, often several, to tear the mussel's byssus threads free from the object. If there is time, strip the byssus from the mussel after you have freed the mussel from its place, discard the byssus, and rinse the mussel off before putting it in the pail. If you are going to cook and serve the mussels the same day, you want them to be as clean as possible. Just as I keep rinsing off and cleaning steamers as I walk home, so I keep rewashing mussels (often in the same pail). It's a matter of habit, and if you commit yourself from the beginning to keep your catch as clean as possible, it will make for both less work later and, more importantly, less grit and sand.

In general, mussels of about three inches long are just right, neither too small nor too big. Once they get too big it is hard to serve them in soup bowls, and if they are too small, there is proportionately less mussel to eat. As you pick them, be sure each is alive. If you can easily open one up, discard it. If one seems heavier than the others—and you will get a feeling for their proper weight very quickly—try opening it, as it may turn out to be filled with sand.

Mussels, which can generally live up to ten years or more, are hardy and can live a long time out of water. While you will probably gather blue mussels from rocks, ribbed mussels are found fully "out" on dry sand during low tide. They can live on shore for a considerable period (after all, they have adapted successfully to living without salt water at all). This gives you more than ample time to find all that you want, though I still think it is wisest to select those that are either partly or wholly submerged just below the tide line. If you do pick off the "dry" ones, simply take extra care to wash them off. The drawback is that they close over more sand or grit on the drier surface if you reach for them there, and they will not open until they are cooked. When you eat mussels, you have a slightly easier task than when eating steamers, as mussels are eaten in their entirety; there is no disposable inner lining, as with the steamer.

Look for mussels where the shore is rocky, at the bottoms of the clumpy peat grasses at the edges of creeks, and in tidal flats, where they are often growing abundantly, sticking out, half buried, or fastened to stones, dead shells, oysters, and other mussels. When you walk through a creek or flat digging for clams at low tide, keep your eyes on the nearby shores so that you can pick up a bunch of mussels on the way home. It takes little time to get all the mussels you need because they are the most easily gathered of all bivalves. And because they are so plentiful intertidally, the odds of finding some are very high. Adding some to your catch after digging steamers or cherrystones can quickly double your total "catch," while adding just a small amount of time to your overall clam outing.

When things happen in nature in predictable ways and patterns, when one set of circumstances naturally leads to another, it is described as "succession." On many of the world's coasts, events occur in such patterns. For example, if oysters get themselves established on muddy, denuded land, their colony will expand. Mussels will eventually attach themselves to the oysters, multiply, and smother the oysters. Then barnacles will arrive and attach themselves to the mussels, multiply, and eventually eliminate the mussels. Succession is taking place.

Mussels fortunately seem to be good at finding new places to congregate. From dark, life-teeming tide pools, to the mud flats, to beds of "thatch" or thick cord grass on the perimeter of saltwater marshes, mussels thrive in different settings and multiply rapidly. Like oysters, it doesn't matter that many of them will be lost, because there are so many of them to begin with!

Mussels that are either at the low-tide mark or just below it grow faster than those that are more fully up on the land, so those you pick from the water will be more quickly replenished. Even though mussels crowd one another out, there are always plenty coming along. The combination of their abundance and their lesser popularity than clams has created a real opportunity for the clammer who wants to diversify his catch.

One of the great pleasures of gathering mussels is that you are spending most of your time at the tide line working leisurely. When you dig steamers, you work rapidly and hard, as the clams are trying to elude you. The mussels, unfair as it may seem, are just sitting there for the taking. They make their one big response to your predation by closing. That's it. Thus you can work at a relaxed pace, taking in all the wonderful variety of the grasses, from the thatch at the edge, to the thick cylindrical stems and the fine grasses, spike grasses, and bullrush. Lauren Brown, well known for her studies of natural grassland communities, has recently called attention to a wonderfully named beach grass that is found only on certain sand dunes, *Ammophilia breviligulata* (Greek for "sand-loving"); early American colonists grazed cattle on it, but stopped as soon as they realized how important the grasses were to sustaining the dunes (see "Grasses and Grasslands of Connecticut" in *Discovery*, vol. 18, no.1, 1985).

Where I gather mussels there is abundant sea lavender and many birds, from a little green heron that always sits hunched up on a sandy point about fifty yards away to Canada geese and tree swallows. Every so often I spot the uplifted head in the water of a diamond-backed terrapin, particularly in the spring when the turtles come to mate in a nearby cove. Musseling is quiet and easy and often leads you to a sense of man as a creature that came up out of the sea. Maybe genetic memory is at work. At the edge of the shore, among the grasses, your feet just into the water, you have a real sense of the eons that nature took to get you there.

SCALLOPS

While there are several hundred species of scallops thriving throughout the world, our principal concern is the popular Eastern bay scallop *(Aequipecten irradians)*, which lives in coastal waters from New England to South Carolina. The scallop has an exotic character, with a delicate taste and many historical associations and uses. The Eastern Bay scallop is found in virtually all colors, and usually in rings of several colors, including bright oranges, whites, blacks, browns, and grays. Its shape is unmistakable with about twenty "ribs" that lead up to the small, beady blue eyes that ring the inside perimeter of the shell and little symmetrical "ears" on each side of the hinge that holds its two symmetrical valves together. The mantle edge is fringed with tiny crimson tentacles.

Like the mussel, the scallop can eject a set of byssus threads to attach itself to objects, often to the bottoms of eelgrasses in which it thrives. It is the rich abundance of sea grasses, and particularly the eelgrass along the Atlantic coast, that makes scallops plentiful—certainly the mainstay of many Shelter Island

Scallop.

families for years. Scallops are typically found anywhere from the low-tide line to water fifty feet deep.

The almost circular scallop shell grows to three inches across and sometimes a bit more. Its distinctive bright blue eyes surround the mantle margin and, although commonly discarded, are considered a delicacy in many countries. You can, in point of fact, eat everything inside the scallop valves, just as you eat the whole oyster or whole cherrystone. Scallops can be eaten raw, though most people don't.

Atlantic bay scallops like the eelgrass and sandy bottoms such as those found in the Peconic Bay, where local scallopers head when the season opens on the third Monday of September. The season continues through April, hence the tradition of scalloping during months with an "r" in their names, which dates back to the days before refrigeration when scallops couldn't be kept easily, and may also relate to their breeding cycle.

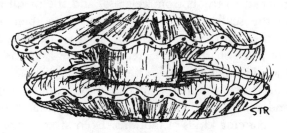

Scallop.

The grasses provide not only sheltered places for attachment, but lots of food and protection from predation. Once the scallops are more mature, and no longer attached, they prefer staying in the grass environment where they developed, which is why "declines in scallop harvests associated with declines in abundance of seagrass meadows have been documented, especially the great 'wasting disease' of the 1930's and 40's" (John M. Foster, "About Seagrass" in *Underwater Naturalist*, vol. 15, no. 2, March 1985).

The scallop's eyes can discern changes in both light and movement, so predation is quickly sensed. This is the key to hunting for it. There are many ways for you to go out and get enough scallops for yourself and friends. Commercial scallopers use large scallop rigs off the sterns of boats. These vessels are equipped with a scallop board along the stern, so that when the net is hauled in and plunked on it, one can stand there and throw the seaweed, eelgrass, and glunk back into the water and pull out the scallops and toss them into the basket beside you. For the individual scalloper, a miniature version of this harness exists and can be manned by one person. You run the harness out behind the boat and drag it along the bottom a short distance, then pull it up quickly. No matter whether commercial or individual, all scallops must be pulled up by hand; it is illegal to pull them up with power—and it used to be illegal even to use boats with power.

Scallops will come up readily if they are around. They are lying on the bottom, or attached to the bottom eelgrass, and the metal bar that runs along the bottom of the scallop dragnet harness will tip them into the net. It is designed to let through those that are too small. The bottom of the harness is usually made of a set of interconnected metal rings, as the sharp edges of the scallop shells would quickly shred a net.

Scallops are free-swimming and can move around with great dexterity. They open and close their valves rapidly, propelling themselves backward, mostly in jerky, dancing kinds of motions. Even after you bring a scallop out of the water, it often sits there opening and closing its shells with a clickety sound, all the time with its eyes upon you—a very different experience from holding the big, inanimate hard-shelled clam in your hand. The scallop is very light in weight because it retains no water, and thus a pail filled with scallops is lighter than, say, one with quahogs.

Another good way to get scallops is to "scap" for them off the end of a boat. Bring your small craft into a part of a bay and use a crab net or, preferably, a clam rake, to get scallops off the bottom. The crab net will eventually wear out, certainly sooner than a clam rake, but it is more efficient because it is wider and easier to manipulate around on the bottom. If it's not too cold, you can also get into the water with a mask and snorkel and pick them up off the bottom, placing them in a bag that is attached to your waist with a lightweight line. Because the scallops move around quickly, grabbing them by hand can be a bit tricky, but it can be done.

I like to go scalloping at low tide on a bright day so that I can reach more of the bottom from the boat. Once the tide starts to rise very far, the areas you can reach become limited. I use a small "scalloper's box," a wooden-sided, glass-bottomed, one-sided box (like a tray with sides) that I rope around my neck and then use to look through to the bottom clearly by placing the glass just below the surface of the water. Once I see that there are scallops around, I cut the motor and drift in the dory, dragging my crab net along the bottom. As I feel it get heavier, I bring it to the surface, usually filled with both scallops and old shells. The metal rim of the crab net works perfectly because it gets underneath the scallops well.

Whether caught by scapping with a crab net or rake, or by using the scallop rig and dragging it like an amateur commercial scalloper, you will find that scallops, in season, and particularly early in the season, are relatively easy to catch. If you get into a section of thick eelgrass, you can find scallops in abundance. As with other shellfish, there is no reason to keep those that are too small. The scallop only lives two years, and its second annual growth ring is at its edge when it is about three inches across.

As discussed in chapter 6, scallops have an amazingly rich and varied set of historical and legendary associations. Both the small bay scallop and its larger relative, the ocean scallop (*Pecten magellicanus*, after the oceanic explorer), are considered one of the best of all seafood delicacies. The flavor of scallops is extremely distinctive, which is why the simpler you prepare it, the better (see recipes in chapter 5). The large ocean scallops, which range up to eight inches, are taken in large numbers in thirty to ninety feet of water by drags off Maine and Nova Scotia.

Because it has no siphons, the scallop cannot burrow down in the sand or mud to escape predation, but instead tries to swim in the opposite direction. If you observe scallops for a while, you will pick up such tricks as tossing a stone or slapping the water in front of them, which startles them into backward flight. You can place your net behind them and they'll come right in. As with crabbing, you are dealing with a sighted creature, a jumpy opponent who moves in ways opposite to your moves, and tries to anticipate you carefully.

Although the rings laid down every year on clam shells do not equate in any systematic way to their age, and simply flatten out as the clams get older, the rings on the scallop, discernible on both valves, are clear indicators of maturity. It is illegal to take the small scallops; take the ones that measure two and a half to three inches from the middle of the winged hinge to the opposite edge of the circle shell.

Because bottom feeders are often preyed upon by starfish, the common starfish *Asterias* may well come up in your net or rake. Commercial scallopers keep them out of the water and thus it is not uncommon to find a pile of decaying starfish somewhere on the shore. They are a major rival to your scalloping effort. Remove them, just as you remove conches and whelks. Although starfish can open scallops more easily than they can open oysters and clams, whose muscles "hold out" longer against the starfish's overpowering suction, the scallops escape more easily by swimming away. When a starfish wraps around a clam, for example, it inserts about a hundred pounds of pressure and opens it just slightly, about one twenty-fifth of an inch. Then the starfish inserts its own stomach into the clam, secreted through its mantle, and proceeds to capture the entire insides of the clam. Starfish are amazing creatures. They also regenerate: if you cut one in half and toss the pieces back into the water, in three months there will be two new whole ones.

Incidentally, swordfish use their long ragged saw to poke around on the bottom and they too enjoy scallops (as well as sea urchins, crabs, and other invertebrates), although you are not apt to encounter one. It is also interesting that scallops have been found at a depth of seventy-two hundred feet in the

Mediterranean. Up until 1840, incidentally, it was widely believed that there was no marine life deeper than eighteen hundred feet.

Because scallops are free-swimming in the more aggressive environment of the open water (as compared with those bivalves that burrow), they are necessarily more alert and quick. Compared with most oysters and mussels, scallops are particularly challenging to catch, and I must admit that there are plenty of days when I have not done too well. In October, however, when I tend to do most of my scalloping, the skies are clear and the foliage onshore just beginning to turn. While you can often combine gathering oysters or mussels with going for clams, scalloping is a different kind of activity and you must make more or less of a commitment to do that and that only. On a clear, bright day in October, it's an easy commitment to make.

5.
Preparing the Catch

Recently I took a bowl of freshly dug steamers to some friends who had invited us for dinner, and suggested that they set them in the refrigerator and enjoy them *à deux* later in the week. The clams were enthusiastically received. The next morning, however, the phone rang, and I was asked, "These are hard-shelled clams, right?" "No," I replied, "these are soft-shelled clams, steamers." This exchange reminded me that there are people who order and happily enjoy eating clams "out" who may never have been told what they are, much less how to prepare them "in."

My aim in this chapter is to make it possible for you to clean, open, prepare, serve, and enjoy clams and other bivalves in the most popular, basic, and traditional ways—steamers with drawn butter, fried clams, clams on the half shell, clam chowders, stuffed clams, fried clams, clam spaghetti, Oysters Rockefeller, Mussels Marinière, and so forth. You will very quickly see how easy it is to prepare clams, as well as mussels, oysters, and scallops. I do not intend to talk about "fixing" clams. The idea of "fixing" food sounds as if it needs to be repaired rather than prepared. Clams need no fixing. They are one of nature's finest food creations, low in calories, high in proteins and vitamins, and extremely delicious. After explaining the basic ways, I offer a section of further recipes.

Preparing clams lends itself either to brooding individual absorption or to the cavalier camaraderie of group cooking in a crowded kitchen. There is not a lot that can go wrong. If you want to be intense about it, that's fine, but it isn't necessary. You don't have to avoid drinking or surround yourself with buzzing timers. A clam cooked too long is, at worst, a little rubbery—but still delectable. Its two valves are either open or in the process of opening so clams can't explode like eggs—or, worse yet, send out one of those little cumulus cloud meringue attachments. A clam won't burn or harden. The truth is—and it is not widely known—it is very hard to ruin a clam.

To cook clams you need to have that often satirized but vitally important newlywed ability to boil water. Granted, things get a little more complicated, but all clams, whether hard-shelled or soft-shelled, as well as mussels and oysters, can be prepared by boiling them in water. If you don't want to get too involved, you can turn on the opera, toss everything into the same pot, and relax until the water begins to boil over. I don't recommend this approach, for each kind of shellfish has a distinctive taste that should be savored, not diluted by a common baptism.

Hard-shelled clams, it should be noted at the outset, fall into three categories, in increasing size, known as littlenecks (after the town on Long Island), cherrystones (after Cherrystone Creek in Virginia), and quahogs, whose American Indian name has been discussed earlier. A "cherry-stone," incidentally, in Shakespeare's day, meant a cherry pit, which in slang meant anything worthless—clearly not meaning clams! In practice, hard-shelled clams fall into two sizes, those small enough to eat raw on the half shell and those whose larger size leads you to steam them open and cut, grind, or chop them to use in various ways. However, the size that can be enjoyed raw varies from one individual to another. Some people feel squeamish about eating anything raw, while others enjoy very large quahogs right out of the shell. Sea gulls, which live healthily and happily for as long as thirty years, often carry a quahog up and drop it on rocks to open and eat it. Because the captured quahog has been stressed, it is tense inside and putting pressure from within on its closed shell, thus making it easier for a predator to burst it open. On more than one occasion I have followed the sea gulls' lead. When I've gotten hungry when out clamming, I have taken two good-sized quahogs and banged them together, then eaten whichever one broke open.

Preparing seafood is a pleasure, perhaps in part because we tend to enjoy seafood dishes more frequently when we are at the shore on weekends or during vacations. Associations vary for everyone, but most of us can probably well recall certain moments of pure joy in encountering both shellfish and other seafood. I think back happily, for example, to the first time early one June that I tasted fresh oysters on the half shell in the streets of Charleston, or the first lobster I ate outdoors on a picnic table somewhere near Bar Harbor, Maine. Some years ago my good friend Ralph, a man of incredible strength, took an eel and skinned it with one long pull, then proceeded to smoke it for a few days. It was the first time I ate smoked eel and I could not believe how fantastic it was.

These and other moments come back vividly simply because seafood tastes so good. Fortunately, there is a great deal of it. Man takes millions upon millions of metric tons of food out of the ocean each year, and while the largest percentage is of finfish, certainly crustaceans, mollusks, and other invertebrates also make their fair contribution to our palates and stomachs. Seafood can be enjoyed throughout the year; you can enjoy steamed clams freshly gathered in the cold middle of March, or make a chowder in December from quahogs you have opened and frozen (and possibly chopped or run through a food processor) late in the summer. To fully understand the joy of shellfish, you need to enjoy it year-round, and with planning and access to saltwater coasts, this can be easily achieved.

People tend to have their favorite ways of doing most things. There are probably as many chowder recipes as there are people who make chowder, and recipes for this and other clam dishes show that regional preferences have endured for a very long time. But there are some fundamental things to know about preparing shellfish. For instance, you need to know that when you eat a steamed clam you can eat everything but the grayish-black "stocking" and when you eat a quahog you leave the white muscle attached to one of the shells, but then again in the scallop, that muscle is the chief edible part—but of course you can eat the *entire* scallop if you want to, and in France the scallop eyes are considered a delicacy. Knowing what shellfish you can eat, and whether you can eat them raw, exemplifies the kind of basic knowledge that you must have to enjoy clams, oysters, mussels, and scallops.

It is a good idea to think carefully ahead of time about how you are going to prepare shellfish because different ways require different amounts of time. This has implications for the timing of your gathering them. For example, if you are going to serve clams cold on the half shell, all you need to do is to allow about twenty minutes to put them in the freezer before you open them. This induces the clams to open slightly, making it easier to run a dull knife or clam opener through them. You can make a cocktail sauce (see p. 92) or cut up lemon wedges while the clams are in the freezer. If you are going to serve clams oreganato (stuffed clams casino), on the other hand, you need to allow time to steam the clams open, grind them, make the stuffing, and bake them, a considerably longer process. In the first instance, you can gather the clams quite close to the time you are planning to serve them, but in the latter you need to get the clams much earlier and, depending on the time of low tide, quite possibly a full day ahead of time.

Just as one more example, consider the timing of gathering and preparing scallops. You can gather scallops during any time of the tidal cycle, though it is generally easier to haul them at low tide when the water is not so deep. Unless you are a semiprofessional scalloper or have otherwise been opening scallops for many years, it takes a long time. It takes a bushel of unopened scallops to yield two quarts opened and ready to eat. So, knowing when you want to eat or serve scallops will tell you when you should gather them, while leaving sufficient time to open them, which takes much longer than opening clams, mussels, or oysters. Try to link the gathering and the preparing of clams and related shell-fish as two parts of a *single* process designed to culminate in a great dining pleasure.

Another general principle to keep in mind about preparing shellfish is that while you cannot really ruin them by overcooking them, they all tend to be best when served less cooked rather than more. Except for large, hard-shelled clams of the quahog size, clams and oysters are most flavorful when eaten raw and icy cold—which is why it is not only attractive but helpful to place oysters or clams on the half shell in a large edged pan or bowl filled with cracked ice. Shellfish can retain the cold temperature well once they are cooled. You can use quahogs that have been refrigerated as mini self-refrigerating units when you take them from one place to another, ideally in a cooler.

As a final general point, try to learn all you can about the waters where you gather your seafood. Information for *all* United States coastal states is keyed in this book's Appendix. There are always local, reliable sources of information to tell you if the waters are or are not good for what you have in mind. Sometimes a change occurs in the water and you need to verify what kind of change it is. On Shelter Island one summer, there was a noticeably brown hue to the water, instead of the normal bluish-green color. People were concerned that this might be a form of "red tide," which contaminates shellfish and which has had a terrible effect on particular coastal areas. Questions were asked—as well they should have been—and authorities quickly reported that the brown color came from a heavy concentration of algae that was harmless to shellfish (or people), and that the sudden change had come about because of an unusual change in the temperature of the water. Once the water reached its more normal temperature, the algae disappeared. In the meantime, people clammed without any fear. The point is, the questions needed to be asked. So you should not only confirm with local authorities the nature of the area you are gathering shellfish in, but ask them about any changes you may observe.

Many people are needlessly fearful that ocean bay waters are unsafe for clamming right after a storm. All storm runoff brings a variety of bacteria into the ocean; however, the likelihood of contamination of the ocean after a storm is very small because the harmful organisms and bacteria do not survive very long in salt water. Bacteria are generally less threatening to clams than you might suspect; clams have an incredible ability to detoxify themselves. It is common practice commercially to dig clams from polluted areas and leave them in cleaner waters for three or four weeks, by which time they are usually then fine to eat. Studies on certain coasts of Italy, where a large amount of debris and bacteria is being put into the waters, found clams to be very healthy despite the water's known pollutants—there may well be some tremendous powers in the clam that we don't yet understand.

You can open clams and other shellfish easily, and can prepare them expertly with very little training. The rules of the game have been around for a long time and for good reason—they work.

STEAMERS

Because digging a steamer is challenging, eating one brings the same kind of satisfaction you get eating a fish caught after a tough fight. If you have been gathering steamers close to when you want to eat them, you may not be able to let them sit in salt water for very long. They will be delicious, although a bit sandy. Steamers in restaurants are apt to be sandy because they have been refrigerated but not kept in salt water, so you have an advantage here by eating them "in." If you can allow for some cleansing time, by digging the steamers on the early side rather than the late side of low tide, for example, the two extra hours for cleaning will be well worth it.

After letting clams clean themselves for a few hours if possible (anywhere up to twelve hours) in a cool, shady spot, you should refrigerate them. If you have large steamers, over three inches, you should refrigerate them more quickly.

86

When you are ready to cook the steamers, here is how you proceed. Rinse them off under cold running water, removing any debris, sand, seaweed, or dried mud that may be on them. Then place them in a covered pot, not quite covering them with water, and bring the water to a boil. Stay in the kitchen so that you can see when the water is about to boil over. At this point, reduce the heat, and let them simmer. When you look at the clams in the pot, you will usually see that some are not fully open (the membrane is not broken). After a few minutes of simmering, the clams are ready. Turn off the stove and let them sit for about five minutes. This allows the froth to settle down underneath them.

The now slightly milky water (clam liquor, as it's called) should be left sitting in the pot as you remove the clams with a large slotted spoon. This is the best way to bring the clams into a serving bowl. If you pour them out into the bowl, or pour the water off into the sink, you are running the water, which now contains a bit of sand and debris, back over the clams, increasing the likelihood of their being sandy, something you have already gone to some effort to prevent.

It is traditional to serve steamers in the following way: Bring all the steamers to the table in one bowl, with a second bowl for the shells you will be discarding. Bring several ramekins of drawn butter, and a pile of napkins. It is not easy for me to choose which moment is more satisfying—getting a secure grip on a steamer and bringing it out of the sand, or dipping the first steamer into drawn butter and bringing it to my mouth. But if you enjoy the one, you will surely enjoy the other.

A few tips about eating steamers. When you pick one up, do it lightly—it's usually still very hot and, like pizza, can be even too hot to handle. Pull the "stocking" off the long siphon, and with it the rest of the thin gray "skinlike" piece, and discard it. Now you can pick up the whole clam by the siphon, dip it in butter, and, holdiing it over a half shell, bring it to your mouth. In this way, by keeping it over a shell, or right on the shell, you will not be dripping butter on everything. Some people use the siphon only to hold the clam, eating just the soft part, but you can eat the whole thing.

I don't think there is any better way to eat steamers than this, but lots of people think that fried clams are best. To prepare fried clams, you proceed as follows: Open the steamers in the same way and remove the stockings. Take the cooked clams and dip them in a raw egg sauce made by simply opening two or three eggs into a dish, adding a little milk, and beating the mixture with a fork. Add a touch of pepper. Dip the clams in the sauce and then into a fifty-fifty mix of bread crumbs and flour. Drop them into a frying pan containing some vegetable oil, and, if you like, a few tablespoons of butter. Let them cook until they begin to get crispy and golden, place them on a paper towel to drain, and serve them either as is or with lemon, tartar sauce, mayonnaise, or seafood cocktail sauce (see p. 92). Tartar sauce can be made easily by mixing ½ cup mayonnaise with one tablespoon each of chopped onions, pickles, parsley, and olives.

The important thing to learn about frying clams is how to keep your fingers from getting overly involved with the flour and bread-crumb mixture, which ends up forming small masses of sticky dough both in the bowl and on the tips of your fingers. The key is to keep the wet and dry steps separate: take the clam in one hand by its neck and dip it once in the bread-crumb and flour mixture, then dip it in the egg and milk mixture, then *drop* it into the bread-crumb and flour mixture a second time and, with your *other* hand, spread a little more of the mixture onto it without touching it, that is, by tossing a little mixture on the top (the bottom is already against the mixture). Then you can drop it into the hot oil and butter mixture.

Another variation is to keep the flour and bread crumbs separate. First take the clam by the neck and dip it in the flour, then dip it in the egg and milk mixture, then toss it into the bowl with the bread crumbs, using your other, dry hand to sprinkle the bread crumbs over it. In this way you have a smoother surface consistency of bread crumbs. The other way, when you mix the bread crumbs and flour together, results in a little surface lumpiness, so it's a matter of preference. In either case, if you don't drag the partly wet clam through the dry mix with the same hand, but instead drop it into the dry mix and cover it with your other, dry, hand, it will work out well. Once you start frying the clams in the skillet, usually you will turn them over in about two minutes. It is a quick process, as the clam had already been cooked when you steamed it open. It will keep cooking when placed on a paper towel to dry. There are many variations on frying clams, but this basic approach will always work well.

Clam fritters can be made with either hard-shelled or soft-shelled clams, and the flavor will of course be different with each. Again, you open the clams in the same way, and then remove them from the pot. Then you cut them in half and mix them with the required ingredients:

Clam Fritters

1 pint opened and minced clams	2 eggs beaten
2 cups sifted flour	1 cup milk
1 teaspoon baking powder	4 tablespoons butter or margarine
1½ teaspoons salt	

Mince the clams. Sift the dry ingredients together. Combine the milk, butter or margarine, and beaten eggs. Add the dry ingredients and stir smooth. Add the clams. Drop the batter with the clams by teaspoonfuls into melted butter. It can take between two and four minutes until they are golden brown. Serves 6 (oysters can be substituted).

Some people enjoy eating steamers raw. For some reason, I've never been one of them. Still, you might want to try them that way at some point. Since the shells are soft and they are not hard to open anyway, it's an easy experiment. It's worth noting, too, that just as steamers can be eaten raw, so can they be used in many of the same dishes as quahogs.

CHERRYSTONES

The hard-shelled clam that we are concerned with here is the northern quahog, or *Venus mercenaria*. It goes by different names: a small cherrystone is a littleneck, and most clam lovers prefer to eat these two smaller sizes as clams on the half shell, although others eat clams large enough to be considered quahogs (over 1½" thick or larger) raw too. There are various published guidelines about the exact sizes differentiating littlenecks, cherrystones, and quahogs, but, as I've already indicated, our concern is with the clam you look at, hold in your hand, and want to eat raw, whatever its size.

Opening a clam by hand is simple once you have learned how. Essentially, you hold a clam knife, or any knife with a straight thin hard blade, in your dominant hand, and place the clam in the other hand. Then you line up the knife along the full edge, sloped toward the narrower end, and push the knife quickly in one motion into the barely discernible crack between the two halves (see illustration, p.91). You can hold the clam on a counter and do the same thing. What is important is *speed* and decisiveness on your first attempt, because if you just rub the knife along the slit, or even bump it casually, the clam literally "clams up" tighter. There are also some good and strong clam openers available. The one made by Hammacher-Schlemmer is my favorite. This handy device allows you to place the clam on a wooden cradle and bring a guillotinelike blade down into the crack between the two halves with greater leveraged strength than you can match by yourself. Be careful not to come

Clam opener.

down too hard, which can result in breaking one or both halves of the shell. There are also some clam openers that work like lobster crackers or pliers that you hold in one hand.

Opening clams is made easier if you place them in the freezer for about twenty minutes. This forces them to open just slightly and makes it easy to get the knife in. If you want to, incidentally, you can simply freeze the clams solid. They will keep this way for a long time. In this case you open them and allow them to sit and thaw before eating them. In general, since they keep easily for as long as five or six days in the lower icebox, just keep them there, then place them in the freezer twenty minutes before you want to open them.

After you have opened a clam, take the knife and run it under the meat on each half, then put both parts on the half shell. When you have a plate full, place your hand over them carefully and pour off any excess water that has spilled onto the plate. In this way you are looking at the perfectly clean meat which has been fully disconnected from the shell. This makes the cherrystones very easy to eat, and guests do not have to begin to eat one and then tug with their teeth to get a part of the clam that is still attached.

Clams served on the half shell are best when icy cold. They can be eaten as is, with a little lemon juice, or with a red seafood cocktail sauce. I like all three ways, and particularly with seafood cocktail sauce, which you can buy or make yourself. The quickest method is to add grated horseradish to ketchup

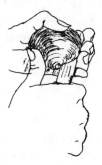
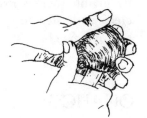

Opening a hardshell clam.

91

until it is hot enough for your taste. A more elaborate sauce can be made as follows:

Seafood Cocktail Sauce

2 teaspoons grated onion
1 finely chopped garlic clove
1 tablespoon finely chopped
    parsley (or parsley flakes)
1 tablespoon grated
    horseradish (or more, to
    taste)

2 teaspoons lemon juice
½ teaspoon soy sauce
    (optional)
1¾ cup tomato ketchup

Combine and mix these together well, varying the amounts of garlic and horse-radish through experimenting several times. Keep the sauce cold in a covered container and make it a day or two ahead of time.

One other point: Look the clams over carefully before you serve them and make sure there are no little pieces of shell stuck to the clams from opening them. Those shells are hard and can really do a job on teeth.

Clams on the half shell are a little richer than steamers and thus you do not need so many. Everyone's appetite differs, but if you serve someone four to six cherrystones, you are usually giving them enough (the same is true for oysters on the half shell), whereas with steamers that would not be nearly enough. Setting out a few plates of opened cherrystones is equivalent to setting out a large bowl of steamers.

QUAHOGS

Because of their size and delicious flavor, not to mention their exceptionally high nutritional value, quahogs form the basis for a wide variety of popular dishes. They are outstanding in chowders, fritters, spaghetti sauce, pies and quiches, as well as in the shell as in stuffed clams and in other ways described later in this chapter under "Further Recipes."

When you bring home quahogs, head straight for the kitchen. There your first assignment is to take out the largest pot you own, ideally either a canner or a tall steamer, and in either case, one with a lid. In general, it is easiest to open quahogs in lesser rather than greater numbers at one time. In other words, open about ten to twelve, remove them, and then open another ten to twelve. It is easier this way because they open more quickly when they are not weighted down by other clams sitting on top of them.

Wash the clams off under running water. You can usually do this easily by hand, but if they have been sitting in the sun for awhile, at the beach, say, they tend to become chalky and you may need to use a brush as well.

Place the quahogs in a single layer around the bottom of the pot, and add enough water to cover them. Bring the water to a boil and then start checking (sometimes you think you are looking through a fog bank) to see if they are open. When they have opened, which indicates that they are fully cooked, remove them with either a large slotted spoon or a pair of tongs. I usually place them temporarily on the turned-over lid of the pot, but you can place them on any clean surface and let them cool. As soon as the pot is empty, repeat the process. The second and consecutive openings will be quicker because you are starting with water that is hotter than with your first batch. Don't try to open too many at once. Piling them up on one another only makes for greater effort in opening and makes it harder to see if they are open. Some quahogs are more reluctant to open than others, and you may even want to remove the open ones and keep putting unopened ones back in their places in the pot. If a clam has opened only partway and I am in a hurry, I insert the closed tongs and open them, forcing the clam to open all the way, thus making it easy to remove the clam. If a clam eventually does not open, discard it.

Opening quahogs is fun. It's more physical than a lot of kitchen activities. You can really get into it: putting clams in, taking them out, boiling, peering into the pot, inhaling clam steam vapors, and spending a fair amount of time at it.

Sometimes the clam comes off the shell, and in fact you need to keep track as you take the shells out of the water to make sure that there is not a loose clam in the broth somewhere before you put in the next batch.

I keep busy with one part of the process at all times. When I have put the next batch of unopened quahogs into the pot, I turn my attention to pulling the newly opened clams loose from the shell, usually by using the tongs. I then drop the clams into a stainless steel bowl and, at some point, ladle a little of the broth into the bowl, which keeps the clams moist (if they sit too long out of water, they will become dry). I usually place either a plastic pail or a large paper bag on the floor near the counter and drop the emptied shells in as I go along, though I save the best-looking, cleanest shells if I plan to make stuffed clams with some of them.

My advice is to do all of them while you are already boiling the water and have the big pot to clean and the mess to clean up. When they are all open, carefully ladle out the broth you want to save from the top of the liquid. This assures that you will not get sand in the broth. This broth can be used both in various recipes and also as a drink, often mixed with tomato juice, which is very nourishing. Let the clams sit in liquid and cool a little so they will be easier to handle.

Now you have several decisions. If you are going to make a clam dish right away, you have to decide how to process the clams—by cutting them on a chopping board or in a wooden bowl with a hand chopper, by putting them through a meat grinder, or by using a food processor. Different approaches lead to different textures. Chopped clams generally go better in chowder and (some feel) fritters, while minced clams are fine for pies, spaghetti, and stuffed clams. You can freeze clams whole in broth (but don't quite fill the container as it will overexpand and the top won't stay on), or you can freeze them processed. Or you can—and this seems ideal—make lots of what you are preparing and freeze what you don't need so that you will simply have to turn on the oven when you want to have that dish again.

In any case, after you decide what you want to do with them, you have them ready to use in any one of a number of great-eating ways. Let's begin with the chowders.

CLAM CHOWDERS

Basically there are three major *types* of chowder: (1) New England clam chowder, generally made with milk and potatoes; (2) Manhattan clam chowder, generally made with tomatoes and vegetables; (3) Rhode Island clam chowder, made with water (rather than milk) and potatoes and often other vegetables. Let's begin with the one I make the most often, a type of New England chowder.

Begin to make the chowder while you are steaming open the quahogs, anywhere from a dozen to twenty, depending on the size. Take a piece of salt pork and cut it into small diced cubes. Sauté them until golden brown, dice one large onion or two medium onions and sauté with the salt pork, and set aside. Peel three or four good-sized potatoes and cook them in three to four cups of clam broth ladled from the top of the large steamer. When the potatoes can be pierced easily with a fork, add the onions, salt pork, salt and pepper to taste, and clams. For chowder the clams are best if chopped, and the more clams the better. Do not boil. Add milk and, if you want to thicken it further, a small amount of flour. If you are going to serve the chowder several times, it is a good idea to divide it before you add the milk. Refrigerate the part you want to save, then add the milk to it when you are ready to serve it again.

Some people like their chowder to include corn. Here's an example. Chop five or six boiled medium-sized potatoes, add four large onions, and cook them in fat generated from diced salt pork in a frying pan. Strip the kernels from five or six ears of cooked corn and add them to the mix, along with the chopped clams and a pint or more of milk. When it comes to chowders there is no reason to be as scientific in your measurements as Fanny Farmer was about everything. Which is why I always keep adding lots of clams, with everything else secondary to the cause.

A Manhattan chowder is red because of tomatoes and vegetables. Here's a delicious way of making it from Shelter Island's Libby Heineman:

Manhattan Clam Chowder

*⅓ lb. of bacon, cut into
  very small pieces*
5 medium onions
4 medium potatoes, cubed
5 carrots
*4 large stalks celery (cut
  vegetables by hand, small
  pieces)*
1 large size can tomatoes

1½ tsp. thyme
freshly ground pepper
*salt (as usual, with
  chowders, taste first,
  clams are salty)*
2 quarts boiling water
*1 dozen or more large
  quahogs chopped in
  blender*

Sauté the bacon until nicely browned on all sides. Remove from kettle. Drain off most of the fat. Add onions and celery. Cook to golden brown. Add boiling water, vegetables, seasonings, tomatoes. Simmer for 1¼ hours or until vegetables are tender. Add clams and juice in the last half hour. Before serving, add browned bacon. Serve with pilot crackers.

Here's another variation on New England Clam chowder, using cream instead of milk, and it comes from Joy McGayhey on Shelter Island.

Boston Clam Chowder

2 dozen fresh clams
1 cup diced carrots
4 cups diced raw potatoes
⅔ cup diced celery
6 cups College Inn chicken broth

4 tablespoons chopped onion
8 teaspoons butter
4 tablespoons flour
1 cup cream
salt and pepper

Open clams. Drain and measure 2 cups liquid (broth). Put carrots, potatoes, and celery into chicken broth, cover, boil gently until tender. Grind clams. Sauté clams and onions in butter, 5 minutes. Blend flour evenly into this mixture. Add broth and vegetables gradually, stirring constantly to keep smooth. Add clam broth, cream, salt, and pepper. Reheat just to boiling and serve. Makes about 16 cups (and it's delicious!)

Clams Oreganato (stuffed clams casino)

Note in the following that it takes about four quahogs to make one stuffed one, and also that the amount of oregano should be varied to individual taste.

4 dozen quahogs
½ cup clam broth
1½ cups Italian seasoned
  bread crumbs
¼ teaspoon garlic powder
  (optional)
½ teaspoon oregano
4 strips bacon

Preheat oven to 400 degrees. Steam open quahogs in covered pot. Remove from shells with tongs, reserving ½ cup clam broth and 1 dozen shells. Coarsely chop the clams by hand or in food processor. Mix chopped clams with bread crumbs, garlic powder, and oregano. Add enough clam broth to make moist. Fill clam shells with clam mixture and smooth the tops. Top each clam with a two-and-a-half-inch strip of bacon. Bake in 400-degree oven until bacon is brown and curled.

Yields one dozen stuffed clams.

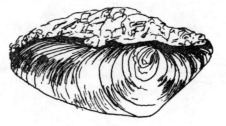

Red Clam Spaghetti (or Linguini or Pasta)

Red clam spaghetti sauce goes extremely well with any kind of pasta. Since Libby Heineman's is so good, once again I choose to share her recipe with you.

2 cups chopped clams	½ teaspoon salt
2 tablespoons olive oil	⅛ teaspoon pepper
2 crushed garlic cloves	1 16 oz. can tomatoes
1 medium onion, chopped	1 6 oz. can tomato paste
3 stalks celery, chopped	½ cup water
¼ teaspoon thyme	1 cup or more clam juice
¼ teaspoon basil	(don't add water)
¼ teaspoon oregano	¼ cup chopped parsley
¼ teaspoon Italian	2 tablespoons butter
seasoning (optional)	

Heat oil in pan. Add garlic and onion and cook until transparent. Add celery and seasonings, add tomatoes, tomato paste, water, clam juice, and parsley. Cook for one hour. Just before serving, add clams and butter.

Serve on spaghetti or other pasta with Parmesan cheese on top (serves four).

Clam Quiche (Impossible Clam Pie)

12 large quahogs
1 cup finely chopped onion
¼ teaspoon pepper
1 cup shredded cheddar (4 oz.)

1¼ cup milk
¾ cup Bisquik
3 eggs
¼ stick butter

Preheat oven to 400 degrees. Steam open clams. Coarsely chop by hand or in food processor. Set aside. Lightly grease 10-inch pie plate. Melt butter in iron fry pan. Cook onions, covered, in melted butter or until soft and slightly browned. Add chopped clams and stir. Spread mixture in pie plate. Sprinkle with cheese. Beat remaining ingredients until smooth (15 seconds in blender or one minute with hand beater). Pour into a ten-inch pie plate. Bake until golden brown, about 30 minutes. Let stand for five minutes. Garnish as desired.

OYSTERS

There's no point in glossing it over, oysters can be very tough to open, and more than one person has cut his hands doing it, and more than one poet has had something to say about it. Shakespeare, in what is possibly the most famous reference to oysters that we have, went at it with a sword: "Why, then/the world's mine oyster/Which I with sword will open." (from *The Merry Wives of Windsor*, II,ii). Lady Mary Wortley Montagu penned these lines, aimed at Alexander Pope, which clearly revealed the difficulty of opening oysters:

> *Satire should, like a polished razor keen,*
> *Wound with a touch that's scarcely felt or seen.*

> *Thine is an oyster knife, that hacks and hews;*
> *The rage but not the talent to abuse.*
> (To the Imitator of the First Satire of Horace)

Pope himself related a wonderful story (which appears in other literary works) which well reminds us that the important thing is to get the oyster opened so that it can be eaten. The following vignette is worth retelling:

> *Once (says an Author; where, I need not say)*
> *Two Trav'lers found an Oyster in their way;*
> *Both fierce, both hungry; the dispute grew strong,*
> *While Scale in hand Dame Justice pass'd along.*
> *Before her each with clamour pleads the Laws.*
> *Explain'd the matter, and would win the cause,*
> *Dame Justice weighing long the doubtful Right,*
> *Takes, opens, swallows it, before their sight.*
> *The cause of strife remov'd so rarely well,*
> *"There take" (says Justice) "take ye each a shell.*
> *We thrive at Westminster on Fools like you:*
> *'Twas a fat oyster—live in peace—Adieu."*
> (Verbatim from Boileau)

The notion of hacking and hewing and the idea of doing it quickly introduce the opposing experiences of opening oysters miserably and skillfully. As with hard-shelled clams, oysters can be opened best when opened most skillfully and therefore most quickly. It's a little like karate in that the force of your move is multiplied by speed.

First, an oyster knife is a good, inexpensive investment and an essential kitchenware item for anyone planning to open a significant number of oysters. Since oysters are known to be somewhat aphrodisiacal, the chances are you will want to continue having them for some time. An oyster knife, which can be

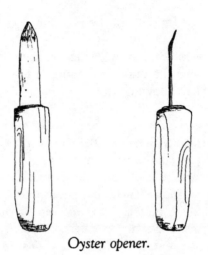

Oyster opener.

purchased easily at most marine hardware or general cookery stores, has a very small bend or curl in the tip, and is made of strong metal attached to a rounded wooden handle that is good for strong gripping. You hold an oyster—and you should, ideally, wear a heavy asbestos-type glove or hold it, flat side up, in a rough towel—in one hand and use whichever hand you normally do things with to manipulate the oyster knife.

All that is required is to insert the curled tip of the knife directly into the pointed, narrow curved end of the oyster, where you will find a very small indentation. This is its Achilles heel, its one vulnerable spot. By inserting the bent tip of the knife there and making a single strong twisting motion with your wrist, you will open the two halves of the oyster. Until you are a bit experienced, the sudden twist may not work perfectly, so simply push the point of your oyster knife in as far as you can and move it back and forth; you will feel it "give" as you sever the adductor muscles. Then you can simply pull the two

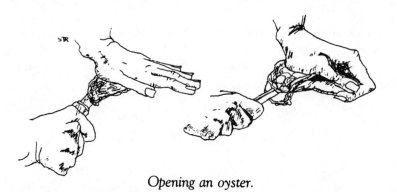

Opening an oyster.

halves apart quite easily. The meat will, as with the clam, cling primarily to one half of the shell, in the oyster's case, the flat side. Run your knife underneath the meat. You now have "shucked" the oyster the right way. The classic wrong way—and believe me, I've tried it—is to use a hammer to bang a screwdriver into the end; usually the other end of the oyster will split. You can open an oyster with a screwdriver, but there is a good chance that you will cut yourself in the process. Despite possible frustration in learning the right way, do not submit to the temptation to simply crush the oyster with a hammer or heavy object from the side. You will make a craterlike hole rather than a neat one, and fill the oyster with shell shrapnel that may make it impossible to eat.

If you are going to serve oysters raw on the shell, you must open them properly, and as with clams, be sure to remove little pieces of shell which may have splintered off and are clinging to the meat. Oysters opened and placed back on their flat shells need nothing more. You can eat them just like that, though most people add either lemon juice or seafood cocktail sauce (see p. 92). The flavor of a raw oyster is very distinctive and different from that of a clam, and because it is somewhat delicate in its taste, it can be more easily hidden by too much of another flavor, so even lemon juice should be used sparingly.

In addition to having oysters raw on the half shell, there are several classic dishes that most people enjoy making. The first is Oysters Rockefeller. For special occasions, you may want to follow the gourmet recipe, but in general the first, quick, and easy way is fine.

Oysters Rockefeller (quick and easy)

2 dozen oysters
2 pkgs. chopped frozen
  spinach
1 bunch scallions (chopped)
½ cup finely chopped celery
¼ cup parsley flakes

8 oz. sour cream
1 tablespoon Worcestershire
  sauce
¼ cup grated parmesan
  cheese
4 tablespoons butter

1. Preheat oven to 450 degrees. Open oysters with oyster knife or by heating in oven on a baking sheet. Keep the deep half of the oyster shell with oyster and liquor in it. Place shells with oysters on baking sheet. One large oyster is enough in one shell, or you may place two or three smaller oysters together in one good-sized shell.

2. Press all moisture out of thawed spinach. Melt butter in a large skillet. Sauté scallions and celery until soft and slightly browned. Mix in all other ingredients except the oysters.

3. Spoon spinach mixture into shells to cover oysters. Bake on a baking sheet for 20 minutes or until piping hot. Two or three oysters make an hors d'oeuvre. For a main course, prepare six per person.

Oysters Rockefeller (gourmet version)

2 dozen oysters
1 pound fresh spinach
  (washed and chopped)
1 bundle scallions, finely
  chopped
½ cup chopped parsley
¼ cup chopped hearts of
  celery

1 clove garlic, minced
6 tablespoons butter
1 cup coarsely chopped
  watercress
1 tablespoon anchovy paste
2 tablespoons pernod
½ cup heavy cream
Tabasco sauce

1. Preheat oven to 450 degrees.
2. Open oysters with oyster knife or by placing on baking sheet in hot oven.
3. Keep each oyster in its liquor in deep half of shell.
4. Melt butter in a large skillet. Sauté celery, garlic, and scallions until tender.
5. Add watercress and spinach. Stir and remove from heat.
6. Mix in anchovy paste, Tabasco, pernod, and heavy cream.
7. Spoon the spinach mixture over the oysters.
8. Bake 20 minutes.

Another popular use of oysters is in both soups and stew, and in these cases you will begin by cooking the oysters first, opening them either by steaming or baking, then separating the shells. Drain them and have them ready for whatever use you plan. Since oysters, like all the other shellfish, are best on the undercooked side, you can generally just add them at the last minute to your liquid dish, but it will not ruin them to include them, say, in a deep dish pie or quiche. The Oyster Bisque recipe is on page 121; here's the stew.

Oyster Stew

3 dozen oysters (shucked,
    liquor reserved)
3 tablespoons flour
4 tablespoons cold water
Dash Worcestershire sauce

½ cup butter
1 quart milk
1 quart half-and-half
Fresh parsley

Blend flour, water, salt, and Worcestershire sauce to make a smooth paste. In a saucepan add paste to the oysters and their liquor. Simmer over low heat with ½ cup butter for about five minutes or until the edges of the oysters curl.

Meanwhile, scald half-and-half and milk. Pour into oyster mixture. Remove from heat and cover. Let stand for fifteen minutes to blend flavors. Reheat to serve, garnishing with parsley. Serves eight.

Scalloped Oysters

1 pint oysters
2 cups cracker crumbs
¼ teaspoon pepper
½ cup melted butter

¼ teaspoon Worcestershire
    sauce
1 cup milk

Drain oysters. Combine pepper, butter, and cracker crumbs. Sprinkle one-third into a buttered casserole, cover with a layer of oysters. Repeat with another layer. Add Worcestershire sauce to milk and pour over contents of casserole. Sprinkle remaining crumbs on the top, bake in a 350-degree pre-heated oven for thirty minutes or until golden brown. Serves six.

Note that fried oysters and oyster fritters are made in the exact same ways as fried clams (p.88) and clam fritters (p.89).

Opening and preparing oysters is challenging but well worth the effort, and guests are more apt to make a fuss over them as the first course. In general, as with cherrystones on the half shell, a half-dozen oysters are plenty for one person, and two or three oysters Rockefeller will suffice.

SCALLOPS

Botticelli knew what he was doing when he placed his famous Venus on a scallop shell. Grace and beauty are in the form and shape of the scallop as well as is an unrivaled delectable quality, and perhaps this explains the extensive use of the scallop in the decoration of much early American furniture, especially on Queen Anne pieces. The scallop is intriguing, delicious, and, unlike the oyster, easy to open.

Here's how. A scallop generally has one side that is covered with a bit of moss and grass and another side that is virtually clean. Place the clean side down in the palm of one hand so you are looking at the mossy shell. Then, with your most coordinated cutting hand, take a plain flat knife and insert it near the hinge, which has a slight aperture. Insert the knife into the opening and run it along the inside of the upper shell. This will allow you to "flip" back the top shell and you will then see what you call a "scallop" or the "eye," which is the single adductor muscle that holds the two halves of the shell together (remember that the scallop swims around by using this muscle to open and close, propelling itself backward). You will also see a bunch of glunk which you probably don't want to eat, though some people do. Take your knife and go around the sides of the "eye," removing everything else. You now are looking at a very clean shell with the white scallop sitting like an island in the middle of it, still attached. Take your knife and cut beneath it, flipping it into a dish as you go. With practice, the movement of inserting the knife, sliding it along the inner shell closely, pulling back the glunk, and then cutting under the remaining white muscle will be executed in just a few graceful motions.

Several other points are worth keeping in mind when you open scallops. Their shells are very brittle, so hold them lightly, not in a strong grip as when you open clams or oysters. Secondly, although frail, their shells are very sharp and, like oysters, can cut you if you are not careful. Also, when you see a stringy piece of green or black glunk on the scallop, remove it with your fingers—not under running water, which removes the flavor.

The most popular, classic way to prepare scallops is by lightly sautéing them in a frying pan. Make sure they are clean, roll them lightly in flour, and drop them into a frying pan with some butter and, if you like, a small amount of white wine. Cook them over a low heat, turning a few times to let them brown very lightly on all sides. It's as simple as that. If you like, you can omit the flour, dry the scallops lightly with paper towels, and sauté them in the same way, but at an even lower heat so that they don't burn. Remember, they hardly need to be cooked at all, and are often eaten raw. They can be broiled by proceeding in the same way and placing them on a cookie sheet in a medium-fired broiler for a few minutes. Again, keep a close eye on them.

There are not a large number of traditional or classic ways of serving scallops beyond the most popular way just described, with the exception of "Coquilles St. Jacques."

Coquilles St. Jacques

There are many different recipes for this most famous of scallop preparations, and they vary in their complexity. In every instance, however, scallops, generally soaked in dry white wine, get combined with sautéed onions and a few spices, then combined with a thick sauce requiring flour. The result is poured onto large scallop shells, usually from ocean scallops sold commercially rather than from the scallops you open, or onto manufactured ones now available. You can also serve them in ramekins or shallow saucers.

No matter how you proceed, you will begin by taking washed, opened scallops and bring them slowly to a boil in dry white wine. You can allow two cups of wine to a quart of scallops. At this point, you can proceed in any number of ways, including this one.

1 ½ pounds bay scallops	*2 tablespoons flour*
5 tablespoons butter	*1 cup heavy cream*
1 bunch scallions finely	*juice of one lemon*
chopped	*4 egg yolks*
12 mushrooms, chopped	*½ cup parmesan cheese*
1 ½ cups dry white wine	*½ cup bread crumbs*

Preheat oven to 450 degrees.
1. Sauté scallions and mushrooms in melted butter until soft.
2. Add scallops and wine. Simmer on low heat two minutes.
3. Pour off liquid into sauce pan.
4. Lower heat and add beaten egg yolks, cream, and lemon juice, stirring continuously. Do not bring to a boil.
5. Stir in scallop mixture. Spoon into ramekins or traditional scallop shell dishes.
6. Sprinkle with parmesan and bread crumbs.
7. Heat about 15–20 minutes or until piping hot. Serves 6.

Coquilles St. Jacques, as is evident from this recipe, is not something to make in a jiffy, but neither is it as formidable as rumored. The taste is more than worthy of its reputation. If you want to take short cuts, you can do all the sautéing and mixing in fewer steps. Simply combine all the ingredients in a mixed-up thick sauce with the scallops in it and then pour it into the shells. This is probably more common than uncommon, but I think understanding the steps helps one understand how the dish builds its character through several stages of preparation. With the ingredients you are using, it is hard to go wrong. Just be careful not to leave them in the oven too long.

MUSSELS

To understand how to prepare mussels you need to orient yourself toward an appreciation of their chief characteristic—the byssus thread by which they move and attach themselves to other objects. This set of byssus threads is usually black and a little thick—they look like a miniature horse's tail—though in certain species in distant parts of the world, as in the *Pinna nobilis* of the Mediterranean Sea, it is a bright golden color. Museum byssus silk (also known as mussel silk) is a very fine textile woven since antiquity from byssus threads. The material is so fine that, according to some, a pair of gloves made of it could be folded up in a walnut shell. It may even be the fabric of the famous Golden Fleece sought by Jason (see *The Oxford Companion to the Decorative Arts*, edited by Harold Osborne). Museums today still display gloves made of this golden material woven into cloth, particularly from the area of the Italian city of Taranto where, in ancient times, artisans busily wove golden cloth from the brightest byssus.

To prepare a mussel you need to remove the byssus completely, simply by holding the mussel from the narrower side in one hand and ripping the threads off with the other. Sometimes this takes several tries as the byssus does not come off all at once. In general, it is best to get a good grip on it and tear it off slowly, as if you were removing a piece of masking tape. I tend to do this when I gather the mussels, but there is not always time, particularly if the tide is coming in and making it harder for you to get the mussels, in which case just keep harvesting and do all the byssus-removing when you're back in the kitchen.

After the byssus has been completely removed, the next order of business is to scrub the mussels under cold running water, usually using a small wire brush. This need not be a particularly arduous task and it need not be over-done. Don't be concerned about removing barnacles. You are only going to eat what is between the shells—an obvious point, but one you may want to re-member when cleaning mussels. No matter how weird or splotchy or covered with other life a mussel is on the outside, the inside is close to pure even before you begin to clean it. Mussels are great breeders of pearls and, even in the small mussels you will be preparing, small, forming pearls are often found. In fact, tiny pearls just beginning to form are not uncommon even in relatively small ribbed mussels. Rivermen on the Missouri River rise early and set down huge iron bars for mussels to grab onto, and then harvest them for their pearls.

After you have washed the mussels well, you can open them in the same way you open steamers. In fact, you can steam them together in the same pot, particularly if you are not intending to save the broth for further use. Mussels will open at about the same speed as steamers, taking from three to five min-utes. They look a bit different in that their inside sometimes swells up into a ball, which comes from their retention of salt water. After the mussels are open (some cooks like to remove the byssus after the mussels are opened, but I don't prefer that timing), I like to let them sit in the hot water for ten minutes, giving them a chance to drain the water a bit, and also because I tend to like mussels just slightly overcooked. In this state they appear a little more mustardy in their yellow hue, as opposed to a yellowish-olive color if you remove them from the water immediately after they are opened.

I prefer eating mussels the same way I like to eat steamers—piping hot and dipping them into drawn butter. Mussels also can be used to make a nice soup. You can simply add them with some of the liquor to milk and thicken with a bit of flour, adding some pepper. You can use mussels in the same way as clams in preparing bisques, fritters, and stews. Some people like to let them sit in a small amount of white wine and nothing else.

Another favorite and easy way to serve mussels is to take a small amount of the liquor from the pot, as with clam broth using a ladle to take the purest part of the broth off the top, and add it to some dry sherry or even a Spanish dark sherry. Then add the mussels to the wine/sherry sauce, warm it over a low heat, and serve it over buttered toast points in broad low soup bowls. The combination of mussels and a small amount of sherry, mixed with the slightly crisp toast that has been buttered, makes for an exquisite meal, and one with a flavor that is truly memorable.

Mussels Marinière (Moules a la marinière)

Many people enjoy making mussels marinière, initially a French dish, and as with Coquilles St. Jacques, you will want to experiment in different ways. Here's how we like to prepare this traditional mussel dish.

Take the scrubbed mussels and rinse them one final time. You are going to be cooking and serving the shells in a sauce so you want them very clean. In a large pot heat some vegetable oil. Chop a good-sized garlic clove into small pieces and sauté in the oil. Put the mussels in the pot and pour in a cup of dry white wine (assuming about 70 mussels, or enough for a first course for four; if it's the main course, make more; incidentally, it's a great opener before shrimp scampi, and since you're into the garlic, why not go all the way?).

Stir the mussels slowly with a large wooden spoon, keeping the mussels attached to their shells. Alternately, you can cover the pot and shake it around a little. I like to see what I'm doing. The mussels will all be open in about six minutes. Some people remove the empty half shells, leaving only the half shell with the attached mussel. I think it's fun to leave all the shells in except any that may have come fully separated. Add either a cup of tomato juice or a six-ounce can of tomato paste and continue to stir. It is great fun to feel the mussels clacking around in the mixture. Sprinkle oregano leaves into the pot and stir. As the mussels begin to open, add a small amount of flour and some seasoned bread crumbs, paprika, onion salt, and more oregano if you like, and keep stirring slowly. The mixture will thicken and work its way completely around the mussel, sticking well to the shells.

Serve the mussels in their shells—which are now partly filled with the thickened red sauce and bread-crumb mixture—by placing them in large soup bowls. This is really a fantastic way to eat mussels. The combination of freshly cooked mussels, wine, garlic, tomato sauce, and a dash of onion is hard to beat for flavor. If it is the principal dish, try serving it with rice, a green salad (with endive, ideally, and a touch of vermouth) French bread (with garlic, of course), and more dry white wine, generally either an Italian soave or a French white bordeaux. One final point—have plenty of napkins or use finger bowls, as the mussels covered with the sauce are going to keep your hands somewhat covered!

HOW TO HAVE A CLAMBAKE

One of the great American traditions, taught by the Indians to the white settlers, is the clambake. It is more than a meal, an event, or an activity. It is to clams and seafood what the Super Bowl is to football. What is it about a clambake that is so sensational? What makes it the superstar of seafood eating?

To understand the "mystique" of the clambake, you need first to stop and ask what it is: clams and other seafood cooked in seaweed on hot rocks. It doesn't sound that overpowering. Hot rocks? Seaweed? But a clambake is special for these very reasons. It is different. It is "roughing it" in a very basic sense. If there were a set of pure polarities in the world of cooking, the clambake would stand at the direct opposite pole from the microwave oven.

Think of the clambake as a process rather than a meal. The first thing to do is to dig a big hole, typically four or five feet long, two to three feet wide, and two feet deep. Ideally you will dig this pit on the beach, and usually a fire department in the area should be consulted first. Then you line the bottom and part of the sides of the hole with rocks, which is why selecting a sandy beach with lots of rocks nearby is ideal. Gather driftwood or scrap wood, possibly throw in charcoal, anything that will burn. Keep the fire going for a good long time, typically four or five hours, all the time letting the coals settle down into and around the rocks. When you have a very hot bed of coals and have maintained it that way for at least several hours, you shovel or rake out and remove all the coals, either burying them in another hole in the sand, or dumping them into the water. Their purpose is over.

You now have a large pit with extremely hot rocks in it. You toss in seaweed, usually the thicker kind with the "poppett" sort of feel to it. As the wet seaweed comes into contact with the hot rocks, a great deal of steam is released, and it is this steam that will do the "baking" of the clambake. You then proceed to put a layer of clams on top of the layer of seaweed. Then cover the clams with another thin layer of seaweed and place more clams of different kinds, mussels, oysters, corn, and lobsters, in each instance mixing in more seaweed. Depending on how many people you have, you just fill the pit, forming a mound with the final seaweed layer, and let everything cook slowly in the hot steam. Onions, corn in its husk, sausages (incidentally, chefs are, increasingly, finding that seafoods and sausages mix well), you can add anything you want to steam, all with the flavor of seaweed and seafood blending in. Depending on how hot you managed to get the fire, it will typically take two to three hours for everything to be cooked. During this period your guests can be involved in other activities, games, drink, talk, while every so often poking into the seaweed to see if the clams have opened and the lobsters turned red. You can use a pitchfork to remove the seaweed when you're ready to eat.

Not everyone has access to a beach, but you can have a clambake in similar style in other ways. On Shelter Island and elsewhere the halves of old oil drums are used, turned upward on their rounded bottoms. You can dig a pit in something other than sand, and if you have enough property and want to have several clambakes a year, you might simply assign a corner of the yard for the purpose. Cooking in a ditch is fun for all kinds of reasons. For one thing, everyone can get involved, which is not true in most kitchens. For another, you are cooking in a sort of primitive way that makes you feel proud. And perhaps most importantly, it's not only a challenge to have a clambake, it's great eating. If you've never done it before, you owe it to yourself to try it soon, and invite some friends to do it with you.

A clambake by process is a group activity, and in slang the term "clambake" has just about become synonymous with any large gathering. In New Orleans, where both shellfish and jazz hold equal sway, a "clambake" is another term for a jazz jam session: with everyone getting together and improvising, this linguistic crossover makes good sense. In slang, a "clambake" sometimes denotes a failure, probably suggesting something chaotic, out of whack—but let's not dwell on that.

One of the most interesting accounts of celebrating a New England clambake in the most traditional ways appears in the July 1985 issue of *Food and Wine*. The authors are true chefs and the photographs will make you hungry. They will probably also inspire confidence. After all, the very worst thing that can happen is that you will not get the rocks hot enough or the seaweed steaming enough and you will take your food indoors and finish cooking it there. In any case, I'll take the deep pit over the microwave any day. It's a way of being in touch with your American heritage. And well before the Indians, many primitive tribes cooked animals in pits, then did the seafood on the coals. Early man would heat stones and then dump them into either carved wooden troughs or holes in the ground containing water as a way of heating the water sufficiently for boiling food. Cooking in pits by the sea awakens a past that is beyond fantasy.

A final note—clambakes have often led to success. More than ten thousand people attended a great clambake in Rhode Island in 1840 on the Fourth of July as a political rally for General William Henry Harrison. That's the good news. Unfortunately, Harrison, our ninth President, who handily defeated Martin Van Buren after the clambake by carrying nineteen of the then twenty-six states, died of pneumonia after only one month in office. But we can't blame the clams for that.

FURTHER RECIPES

Given the length of time that man has been eating clams and other bivalves, and given human interest in diversity, it is likely that the number of ways of preparing them is close to infinite. Certainly new ways stretch before us into the future. You should not be timid about experimenting. While many wonderful dishes have been created, I firmly believe that the firmament has room for many stars. While I eat most of my clams in the traditional ways already explained, I nevertheless think it is fun to do some different things once in a while. Toward that end I offer a recent experiment as an example of how you can break new ground, and then conclude with some other good recipes you may want to try.

Last summer I tried making something I can best call "Clams and Mussels Marinara." I decided it would be fun to cross the best of both worlds by combining steamers with mussels marinière (p.112). Thus I created the mussel sauce in the same way, set it aside, then steamed open and shucked four dozen soft-shelled clams. Then I cooked the mussels in the sauce, leaving them in their shells. Then just before I served the mussels, I added the shucked steamers to the sauce and stirred them in as well. Suddenly I had a combination that was fantastic and was eaten about as rapidly as any seafood dish I've served.

Just as combining steamers with mussels marinière resulted in a new dining venture, so can many other "cross-pollinations." You can stuff an avocado or cucumber with clams, oysters, or mussels and top with a light mayonnaise sauce or just mayonnaise itself (as is increasingly popular with cold salmon). You may have been making different kinds of meat hashes, so try a hash made with chopped clams and onions. Try some things with clams you may have first tried with fish. For example, a bluefish lightly covered with lemon and sprinkled with nutmeg, then baked, is delicious. Maybe nutmeg would go well on mussels. That people have enjoyed experimenting is obvious from the further recipes offered here.

White Clam Sauce

Open and shuck several dozen hard-shelled clams. Save the liquor and chop the clams. Sauté 2 or 3 cloves of chopped garlic in pure olive oil (approximately ¼ to ½ cup). Do not brown the garlic as it will become bitter. Add clam liquor, chopped parsley, and black pepper (red pepper if desired), and simmer approximately 10 minutes. Add chopped clams, the more the better, and cook for only 2 to 3 minutes. If you cook it too long, the clams get a bit tough. Pour over hot spaghetti or linguini. The exact proportions of spices will vary to taste.

Clam-stuffed Mushrooms

2 lbs. mushrooms
1 pint of shucked, chopped
  clams
½ cup butter
1 clove garlic (minced)

½ cup dried bread crumbs
⅓ cup chopped parsley
¾ teaspoon salt
¼ teaspoon pepper

Remove stems from washed mushrooms. Place caps with the round side down on a broiling pan or baking sheet. Drain the clams and reserve the liquor. Melt butter and brush into caps. Cook chopped stems and garlic in remaining butter and a little clam liquor. Cook until tender. Mix in chopped clams and all other ingredients. Spoon mixture into mushroom caps. Broil approximately 8 minutes or until caps are tender.

Oyster Pie

This delicious pie comes from my wife's grandmother, Mary Travis. One quart of shucked oysters. Rich biscuit dough. Line the sides of the baking dish with dough; place a small cup right in the center of the dish (allowing for expansion room later). Fill the dish with oysters. Sprinkle over the oysters flour and some small bits of butter. Season with salt and pepper. Cover the dish with hot oyster juice. Remove the cup, creating a well. Cover the dish with biscuit dough and bake for about forty minutes at 350 degrees or until dough is lightly browned.

Scalloped Oysters

3 dozen oysters and liquor *2 cups finely rolled crackers*
(½ pint) *2 cups milk*
1 teaspoon salt *½ cup butter*
few grains of pepper

Remove any bits of shell from the oysters. Strain off the liquor and save. Add salt and pepper to oysters. Alternate layers of oysters and cracker crumbs in greased baking dish. Combine milk, butter, and oyster liquor; heat until butter is melted. Pour into baking dish. Bake at 350 degrees for 45 to 50 minutes. Serves six (from Mrs. Dorothy Webster).

[These next four wonderful Italian recipes come from Camille Mastrogiovanni of New Haven, and I know you'll enjoy trying them].

Zuppa Di Clams

Sauté 2 or 3 cloves of chopped garlic in approximately ½ cup of pure olive oil. Don't brown the garlic because it will become bitter. Add well-scrubbed clams and/or mussels to sautéed garlic. Add chopped parsley and dried red pepper (if desired). Cover pan and steam clams. Cook only until clams are steamed open. Salt and pepper to taste, and pour over linguini or spaghetti (clams are left in the shell).

Clam Pizza

Roll out your favorite pizza dough. You can use a round pan for pizza slices or an oblong pan to cut pizza into small squares for hors d'oeuvres.

Sprinkle the dough liberally with chopped garlic, chopped parsley, coarsely chopped clams, grated parmesan cheese, and black pepper. Drizzle pure olive oil over pizza.

Place in preheated 450-degree oven. Bake approximately 15 minutes, then lower heat to 350 degrees and continue baking. This should take approximately 30 to 40 minutes' total time, depending on shape and size of pan. Cut and serve piping hot.

Stuffed Clams Casino

24 littleneck clams
1 medium size bell pepper
¼ cup grated parmesan
  cheese
½ oz. dry sherry
24 squares mozzarella
  cheese (¾" sq. × ⅛"
  thick)

4 strips of bacon (each strip
  cut into 6 pieces to make
  total of 24 pieces)
2 cloves garlic (finely
  chopped)

Wash clams. Open clams and place on baking platter. Pour juice from clams into platter (not on clams).

Mix together pepper, garlic, cheese, and sherry. Put approximately ½ teaspoon on each clam. Place slice of bacon and mozzarella on top of each stuffed clam. Sprinkle with bread crumbs and chopped parsley.

Bake at 400 degrees for 10 to 12 minutes. Place baked clams under broiler until browned.

Scungilli

For those of you who don't want to throw those large conches and whelks back or remove them as clam predators only by tossing them on the beach, you might want to consider this traditional Italian way of preparing them. The key is to slice the pieces very thin and even to pound them a little in order to soften them up.

Scrub the conch or whelk shells; it's important to clean them well. Place in a pot of boiling water, enough to cover the shells. Boil for 30 to 45 minutes. Cool. Pull the meat out of each shell, using a fork (like getting the tail meat of a lobster). Cut off the "soft" end and discard. Slice the remaining, firm meat very thin.

Seasoning: pure olive oil, finely chopped parsley, finely chopped garlic, salt and pepper to taste, freshly squeezed lemon juice. The quantities depend on how many animals you have, and on their size. You'll need to experiment, and I suggest you start by cooking and slicing a few, then varying the spices. Chill and serve with lemon wedges.

Oyster Stuffing

½ cup celery, chopped
½ cup onion, chopped
¼ cup butter
6 cups dry bread crumbs
1 tablespoon parsley,
  chopped

3 cups oysters, chopped
salt and pepper sprinkled in
2 eggs, beaten
1¾ cup milk and oyster
  liquor mixed as you want

Cook celery and onion in butter until browned. Add crumbs and parsley. Mix. Add oysters, seasonings, and eggs. Add enough liquor to moisten.

Oyster Bisque

4 cups milk
1 onion, grated
3 teaspoons salt
¼ teaspoon white pepper
1 ½ pints oysters

1 cup water
5 tablespoons butter
4 tablespoons flour
½ pint heavy cream,
   whipped

Grate the onion into the milk. Sprinkle in salt and pepper and bring to a boil. Place clean oysters and their liquor in a separate sauce pan and bring to a boil. Let oysters simmer until edges curl (a general rule about cooking oysters). Strain liquor into the milk and chop oysters coarsely in chopping bowl.

Melt butter in double boiler. Blend in flour. Strain milk into flour mixture, stirring constantly to keep smooth (the goal in a good seafood bisque). Add the chopped oysters and keep stirring. This can now be set aside for 24 hours, bringing out the flavor of the oysters more fully. To serve, reheat over boiling water. Serve in bouillon cups. Garnish with whipped cream that has been slightly salted, add a little chopped parsley and a dash of paprika for decoration. Serves eight to ten.

(As a final offering, the next two recipes come once again from Shelter Island chef Libby Heineman.)

New England Clam Pie

Pastry for 1 crust pie
2 dozen soft-shelled clams
    (steamers); chopped
    quickly in blender
¼ lb. salt pork or bacon,
    diced
2 medium onions, chopped
    fine
2 carrots, diced fine

½ cup water
3 potatoes, diced
2 cups clam liquor
piece of bay leaf
1 small garlic clove, crushed
dash nutmeg, dash fresh
    pepper, ½ teaspoon salt
1½ tablespoons flour

Fry salt pork or bacon until crisp. Remove and save. Sauté the onions and carrots in drippings until lightly browned. Add water and simmer a few minutes. Add potatoes and clam liquor. Cook until vegetables are tender. Add the chopped clams. Season with bay leaf, garlic, nutmeg, salt, and pepper. Thicken with flour made into a smooth paste with a little water. Cook a few minutes. Cool slightly and pour into a 1½ quart casserole. Cover with pastry crust, gashed for steam. Bake in very hot oven, 450 degrees, until crust is brown, from 25 to 30 minutes. Serves six.

Towd Point Clam Pie

1 doz. hard-shelled clams
   and juice
1 large onion
3 tablespoons butter
2 tablespoons flour
1 cup milk
¼ teaspoon salt
⅛ teaspoon pepper
¼ teaspoon paprika

Chop onion and sauté in butter until yellow; add flour and smooth. Add milk and clam juice and cook until thickened. Chop clams and add seasonings. Put between unbaked pie crusts and bake in hot oven (450 degrees) until crusts are brown, from 15 to 20 minutes. Serves four.

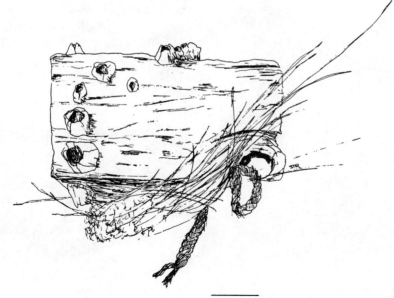

6.
Clam Trivia

Anyone with my passion for clams and clamming should probably not even whisper that there is anything trivial about the subject. Still, one need reckon with the way of the world, and there is a certain force about the recent interest in trivia demonstrated by our society that suggests I cannot, without risking the sale of my book, exempt myself from being a participant. Fortunately, there is a wealth of interesting information about clams and other mollusks, and this final chapter is a kind of catchall that follows the real catch.

The Life Span of Clams
Man has always been interested in how long various creatures live. It is a logical extension of our concern for our own mortality. We ourselves are relatively long-lived, enjoying a typical life span of seventy years, and the figure seems to be rising steadily. Other animals that live relatively long are elephants, alligators, giant salamanders, hippos, rhinos, gorillas, whales, and certain kinds

of fish. According to F. Kendig and R. Hutton, authors of the very fascinating *Life-Spans or How Long Things Last* (New York, 1979), the only creatures to live longer than man are tortoises, turtles, *the European freshwater clam,* some bacteria, and some simple, uncomplicated creatures like sea anemones and sponges.

The clam is the surprise. Kendig and Hutton note that the European freshwater clam is the longest-living invertebrate, known to live up to 116 years. Clams found in United States waters have been proven to live up to 60 years, and recent research suggests even much longer, possibly 150 years. The giant clam, whose shell can weigh over five hundred pounds, typically lives about 30 years. As noted earlier, it takes about seven years for a clam to reach the size to be harvested, and the "rings" on the outside of the clam valves are not precisely correlated to years but they do represent growth. Our friend the quahog is the longest-living mollusk. In eastern seas there is a very large shell mentioned in Frazer's famous *The Golden Bough* which is known as "the old man." On Fridays certain natives apparently turn the shells upside down on the thresholds of their houses, in the belief that *their* own longevity will be improved.

A few related points about longevity: Minnows typically live a year whereas sturgeons can outlast man. American eels grow slowly, typically live anywhere from 7 to 20 years, and have been known to reach 60 years in captivity. Hermit crabs go for about 11 to 12 years, blue crabs from 2 to 3, Dungeness crabs on the West Coast, 8, Alaska King crabs, over 15. The longest-living crustacean is the good old lobster. A 35-pounder might be 50 years old. The largest lobster on record weighed 44.5 pounds. The one you typically eat, 1.5 pounds if you are lucky, is about 7 or 8 years old.

The Man-Eating Clam

Let's go back to that giant clam. We've all heard the stories about divers being trapped by giant man-eating clams. The stories are not true. There is no known documented case of a man's being killed in the closing valves of a clam, probably because the giant clam's shells close very slowly. In Maori legends, the one of "Rata's Voyage" tells of a man named Ngana who is hired (because he had once concealed himself in a gourd and promised to kill sea beasts) to kill a giant clam believed to be preparing to close on a canoe—not very likely, since the giant clam doesn't get off the bottom! Known as *Tridacna gigas*, the giant clam of the South Pacific sits on the bottom, like many other clams. Like most oysters, it is sessile, or stationary. It feeds on the microscopic life produced by affixed algae with which it has a symbiotic relationship. The giant clam's shell, typically weighing some 300 pounds, with its large fluted edges, is a beautiful object and was often used for baptismal basins. According to the *Guiness 1984 Book of World Records,* the largest bivalve we know of is a giant clam 43″ by 29″, weighing 579 pounds. It was collected from the Great Barrier Reef in 1917. You can see it today in the American Museum of Natural History in New York.

Largest Pearl from a Clam

W. J. Cronin notes in *The Living World of the Sea* that one giant clam yielded a 14-pound pearl in the Philippines. Given the weight of that one, we would have no trouble accepting the biblical directive, "Cast not your pearls before swine" (Matthew, 7:6).

Biggest Appetite for Clams

Guiness also notes another record relating to clams: the eating record is apparently 424 littlenecks in 8 minutes by David Barnes at Port Townsend Bay, Washington, May 3, 1985 (you might also be interested in knowing that someone in California ate 17 bananas in two minutes, and I, for one, think that record would be easier to beat than the littlenecks).

The Smallest Clam

We know a bit more about the giant clam, the largest of all bivalves to have evolved, than about the smallest clam, but Grizimek, in his very readable *Animal Life Encyclopedia* (New York, 1974), writes that the smallest bivalves known are in the interestingly named *Fingernail Clam* (or *Pisidium*) group. Some of them choose not to be anywhere near the bottom but in fact hang vertically from the surface of the water. They have been found in deep water and in Alpine lakes 2500 meters high that are frozen most of the year.

Shellfish Farms

Marine aquaculture, the underwater farming of sea creatures, has been going on for thousands of years. We know from Pliny that as early as 100 B.C. the Romans were farming oysters grown commercially. Today there is worldwide experimentation in shellfish farming. In the northwestern part of the Black Sea they are working on mussel aquaculture. In New Zealand they are trying out scallop-farming methods based on the experiences of Japan. In Tasmania, an oyster farmer is successfully growing oysters inside bags on his lease near the mouth of the Dutch River. Both hard-shelled and soft-shelled clams are farmed and harvested on both the Atlantic and Pacific coasts. All the popular bivalves, not surprisingly, are being seeded and farmed. From France and Spain to the Mississippi River, mussels are being grown on everything from ropes to stakes interwoven with brushwood to metal tongs. This is not surprising, for man is in love with bivalves, and has been since prerecorded history.

Commercial clamming, an important part of our national economy, has been going on for a long time, and researchers work side by side with those in the industry to improve the yield. Particularly extensive work has been undertaken on the southern Atlantic coast, and one impressive document is entitled "Exploratory Clam Survey of Florida Nearshore and Estuarine Waters with Commercial Hydraulic Dredging Gear." Written by Mark F. Godcharles and Walter C. Jaap, this is Professional Paper Series #21, October 1973, published by the Florida Department of Natural Resources, the Marine Research Laboratory at Saint Petersburg. I give you the full reference in this case because the study is not only fascinating but well captures earlier studies and contains an excellent bibliography covering numerous commercial clamming activities along the Atlantic. It is a good beginning point for anyone who wants to look extensively into the subject. Incidentally, if you come across seed clams, which of course you can't keep, there is nothing to prevent you from placing them in a spot where you can look for them again when they have grown larger.

scope of what is involved when you grow
he following, as summarized in the 1981
and June 14, 1980, four oyster reefs in Mis-
Alabama, totaling 792.6 acres, were planted
am shell, in densities ranging from 99.6 to
r acre. Or again, one large bed of mussels off
as so filled with other kinds of life that a 10"
ut only 625 were mussels! (Cronin, *The Liv-*

Red Tide

een centered around three clams, the northern
nd the sunray venus clam *(Macrocalista nim-*
about their findings, but about how the "red
tide can make an effect act on clamming. I share their statement with you here as an illustration of the red tide's impact: "1800 marked the beginning of commercial southern quahog harvesting from the Ten Thousand Islands, at one time the location of the most productive and extensive clam bed in the United States. . . . Harvesting in this area with mechanical conveyor type dredges began in 1905, continued until 1947 when production fell from a peak of 1800 bushels to fewer than 200 bushels of clams per day. . . . Coincident with this decline was the 1946–47 red tide, the most devastating outbreak ever

recorded for Florida. Many fishermen believe this red tide was responsible for the decline of the Ten Thousand Island quahog fishery."

Red tide is a tremendously threatening event in nature that wreaks havoc with sea life but which fortunately does not occur too often or too gravely. All we know is that for some reason the south wind stops every few years and a wind from the north moves down. It is called *El Niño*, meaning "the child," because it often comes near Christmas time. A large-scale set of ecological changes came about in the Galapagos Islands during the El Niño of 1982–1983. For example, the Galapagos marine iguanas died by the hundreds when they were suddenly deprived of their normal meal of sea lettuce—which had been dramatically reduced by the unusually warm surface water. Penguins swam hopelessly into Academy Bay off Santa Cruz, something that had not happened since the last El Niño, in 1972. For species with poor mortality, unlike most sharks, which simply disappear for a while, El Niño can literally put an end to them. It keeps the waters that are close to shore from moving out, and, deprived of the cooling Humboldt current, the waters get warm, stagnant, and loaded with unusual plant life. Together they create a red tide. Birds become confused and try to migrate, but many die on the shore and their decaying bodies make the water even worse. Eventually there is a change and everything that had been kept out of the waters comes at once. Thousands of hammerhead sharks can suddenly invade southern waters when the change occurs. Birds and dolphins come in droves. The south wind resumes, the inshore waters move out, the temperature drops, and things return to normal. The interim period can be absolutely terrible on all sea life, including clams.

Curiously enough, laboratory rats, when fed the same microscopic dino-flagellates which in abundance cause "red tide," thrived well on it. The single-cell organism, *Gonyaulax polyedra*, which wreaks havoc on shellfish, apparently contains up to 26 percent protein and includes all the amino acids necessary for nutrition (as reported in *Sea Frontiers*, vol. 14, no. 5, 1968).

All this is not to say that everyone should be upset, however, when the waters in one's area turn color or fill with algae. There are often periods of change and most of them are not long-lasting enough to harm clams or other sea life. Remember, too, that the huge Amazon River, which flows some 4,000 miles, is brown from the sheer force with which it moves through the continent, and it causes the ocean waters to remain brownish for about 150 miles outside the mouth of the Amazon.

Clams in Myth and Legend

As far as I can tell, there are no references to clams in the Bible. And despite the fact that clams have been used as tools, decorations, and instruments of barter from early times, there do not seem to be many references concerning them in mythology. One related exception: there is a genus of mollusks known as *Leda hamata* (hooked leda), named after Leda, who in mythology was impregnated by Jupiter who visited her in the form of a swan. She consequently gave birth to Castor and Pollux.

"The Clammer," *by William John Hopkins, 1906.*

A wonderfully rich and enjoyable turn-of-the-century novel was written about a clammer and probably represents the only full treatment of clamming in an American work of fiction. Entitled *The Clammer*, this novel was written by William John Hopkins and was published in 1906 by Houghton Mifflin and Co. The novel is told in the first person by Adam, a clammer who falls in love with the rich man's daughter, of course named Eve. He wins first her and then her father by getting them excited about the clams he digs out on the mud flats. The novel contains excellent descriptions of clamming and several clambakes. Here is how Hopkins describes how the rich man of the town gets into clamming: "And Old Goodwin, after further searching in the tree, drew forth a clam hoe and a basket; and being thus equipped, he hied him to the flats, which were, by now, almost bare, and he began to dig. Now that is a luxury which the rich may seldom have, that they should dig for clams. Old Goodwin enjoyed it mightily, splashing here and there in his boots, and digging as the fancy seized him; which was as like to be where the clams were not as where they were. But he cared not at all, and drew long breaths for very joy of living; and the clams that he found he put within his basket."

Despite a hurricane, hard winters, and a recalcitrant future mother-in-law, Adam triumphs, wins his love, and plans to spend all his days clamming. The author's great enthusiasm for clams comes across well in this description of a clambake: "The hole was scooped in the ground and lined with great stones. And on these stones I kindled a fire that roared high; and when it had burned long and the stones were hot, I raked the ashes off. Then I shook down upon the stones fresh seaweed from the pile, and on the seaweed laid the clams that I had digged, myself—and alone—that morning. Then, more seaweed; and the other things, in layers, orderly, with the clean, salt-smelling weed between: the lobsters, green and crawling, and the fish, fresh caught, and the chicken, not too fresh, and the sweet and tender corn, and sweet potatoes. And over all I piled the weed and made a dome that smoked and steamed and filled the air with incense." Certainly a "high" moment for all who enjoy gathering and eating clams!

Clammy Names and Other Trivia

As far as individuals with "clammy" names, there is not so much to reveal as in the case of geography. There is a Clam Gulch, Alaska, but not much in the phone book. However, for Ron Vanden Dorpel, who has a keen interest in military history, let me point to Count Eduard von Clam-Gallas (1805–1891), an Austrian general who did well in Italy and Hungary (1848–1849), was engaged at Magenta and Solferino (1859), and in the Austro-Prussian War (1866), but alas, suffered four defeats later on and was relieved of his command and retired. Count Heinrich Jaroslaw von Clam-Martinic (1826–1887), however, was an Austrian politician who fared better and whose nephew Heinrich (1863–1932) served as Austria's prime minister (1916–1917). Now that's trivia. As is the fact that the largest known mollusk eye is that of the giant squid, which measures about the size of an L.P. record, and that the West Coast Indians used the Pismo clam *(Tivela stultorum)* as their unit of bartering equivalent to the East Coast Indians' "wampum."

Clams in Archeology

Paleolithic man frequently turned to animals for his art work, in various media, and it has been quite common, over the years, for archeologists to unearth skeletons bedecked with bracelets, headdresses, and other symbolic and artistic, decorative ornaments made from shells. We know a great deal from the diggings in funeral sites and burial grounds, as well as from the analysis of huge shell mounds (also known as "kjokkenmoddings") such as those discovered in Spain at Mugem in the Valley of the Tagus. There, about 2025 meters above the present sea level, archeologists discovered gigantic heaps of marine shells, including those of oysters, whelks, scallops, razor clams and cockles. Prehistoric archeology is filled with such stories.

In the later neolithic period our ancestors used "limpet hammers," generally made out of flint, to bang shellfish off rocks. This has been particularly well documented through the exploration of shell remains along the western coast of Scotland. We also know about our ancestors' love of shellfish from the "middens" or large rubbish heaps they left behind them. Shellfish remains are very plentiful in these piles, as are fish bones and bird bones. From these middens, archeologists learn about prehistoric man's diet, economy, community size, and travel. They also have literally unearthed information on how clam shells were used in giving clay a greater body in pot-making. In the midlands in England, for example, a certain "shell-gritted" pottery ware was very popular in the third century. The uses of shells are incredibly diverse throughout history.

Of wonderfully rich background is the use of the "cockle" in history and literature, with various byways and folklore taking us well beyond the simple story of sweet Molly Malone selling her "cockles and mussels alive, alive, o!"

"Cockle" is from the Latin *conchylium*, the word for conch shell, and the phrase, "to warm the cockles of your heart," meaning to feel deeply, has no connection to the bivalve. Rather it refers to the Latin *cochleae cordis*, or ventricles of the heart.

In the late 1920s the well-known archeologist, G. H. Luquet, reported that the Abbé Ducrost at Solutré had found an ancient skeleton decorated with different shells, including a large valve of the scallop, *Pecten jacobaeus*, pierced near the hinge. Obviously special significance and possibly protective symbolism were attached to the shell. In more recent history, the exact same shell became known as "The Pilgrim's Scallop" because it was worn in the hats or on garments of many crusaders returning from the Mediterranean. In particular, many pilgrims who traveled to Santiago (St. *Jacob*) de Compostela in Spain wore this shell, and the popular and the scientific names derive from this fact.

In the early eleventh century people became excited over the discovery of the tomb of St. James the Apostle, who reportedly had been beheaded in Palestine and transported to Galicia, the Celtic region of northwest Spain. Adjacent to this tomb were founded a church, a monastery, and a shrine. The city was heavily associated with scallop shells because pilgrims coming there wore the shells in their hats. In Salamanca, there is a famous fifteenth-century house, "Casa de les Conchas," which was built by a Doctor Talavera Maldonado, a Knight of Santiago, who had all the facades of the house decorated with scallop shells like those of Santiago. In Shakespeare's time a "cockle hat" meant the hat of a pilgrim, and scallop shells on a hat symbolized St. James of Compostela. The polished side of the shell was frequently decorated with religious drawings, and sometimes the shell was taken out of the hat and used as a water cup. In any case, it was also meant to ward off evil spirits, just as it had been used millions of years earlier in the funeral sites.

Sir Walter Raleigh wrote, in his "The Passionate Man's Pilgrimage," "Give me my scallop shell of quiet, My staff of faith to walk upon . . . And thus I'll take my pilgrimage." Ophelia echoes these lines in Shakespeare's *Hamlet:*

Clam Trivia

How should I your true love know
From another one?
By his cockle hat and staff,
And his sandal shoon.
(IV, v, 23)

The scallop's symbolic uses evolved further after Raleigh's day as it became used increasingly in the decorative arts, ranging from family coats of arms, to drawers on Queen Anne lowboys, to its use as the Shell Oil company's shield. Perhaps Botticelli's depiction of Venus arising from the sea on the scallop shell, a huge and wonderful painting that today hangs in the Uffizi in Florence, Italy, inspired other artists to grasp its uniquely beautiful lines.

Exterior wall of Salamanca's House of Shells, Spain.

Clamor

There is, as one might suspect, a relationship between the words "clam" and "clamor." Bells provide the link. In a church belfrey, when bells are "clammed," they are all pulled at once, bringing the melody to a stop in a resounding "clamor" of sound. The *Oxford English Dictionary* cites some anonymous lines of about 1800 referring to the Belfrey in Saint Peters, Shrewsbury: "When bells ring round and in their order be, They do denote how neighbors should agree; But when they *clam,* the harsh sound spoils the sport, And 'tis like women keeping Dover court." It seems that, as in slang, to clam up means to become quiet, so to "clam bells" is to silence them, but not without the "clamor" in between!

Oysters in Literature

Few of the world's great authors have neglected to refer to oysters, in either figurative or literal ways. Consider Shakespeare in *As You Like It,* "Rich honesty dwells like a miser, sir, in a poor house, as your Pearl in your foul oyster" (V,iv,63). Or Chaucer in his Summoner's Tale (line 392), "Many a Muscle and many an oystre, when othere men hath been full well at ease hath beene our foode." In slang one hears the expression, "And did you ever see an oyster walk upstairs?" as a retort to someone who is exaggerating. The phrase "close as a Kentish oyster," as well as many similar phrases, is used popularly to mean tight-lipped, and the same holds true of many references to clams. When Bunyan wrote his *Apology for His Book,* he commented, in mocking self-effacement, "If that a pearl may in a toad's head dwell, And may be found too in an oyster shell."

Clamshells for Long Island in 1661

I was interested to learn what the Indians were actually paid by the white settlers for *all* of Long Island. Here, reportedly, is the price tag the Dutch gave to the Indians when the purchase was made in 1661:

6 rugs	12 lbs. flour
10 coats of duffell	30 lbs. lead
30 lb. kettle	3 dozen knives
60 strings wampum	12 cans brandy
10 hatchets	1 half-barrel beer
8 adzes	10 lbs. tobacco
2 guns	

This was quite an exchange. Of course the wampum should not be noted lightly. The "strings" referred to were usually each a fathom (six feet) in length. As their first supply of it, the Pilgrims bought about 200 strings of wampum (known as "roanoke" by the English in Virginia). This supply allowed the Plymouth settlers to have a virtual monopoly on the fur trade in New England for several years. Wampum's value cannot be underestimated. William Bradford wrote: "But that which turned most to their profit in time was an entrance into the trade of Wapmumpeake (the Indian wampumpeag, meaning white strings of money), for they now bought about £50 of it of them; and they told them how vendable it was at their forte Orania [Fort Orange, now Albany, New York], and did perswade them they would find it so at Kenebeck . . . and afterwards, they could scarce ever gett enough for them for many years togeather" (from G.F. Willison, *The Pilgrim Reader*, New York 1953). Bradford goes on to describe its scarcity, and how many people wore it, how the Naragansetts and Pequents made and kept the most, allowing them to remain very rich and powerful.

Eventually other tribes caught on and copied the Naragansetts, "and it hath continued a current commoditie about this twenty years [until 1647], though it may prove a drugg in time." In any case, it was a lot easier to deal with and handle than corn, the previous trading commodity of the Pilgrims. The white beads were usually from whelks and the purple from quahogs. There were thousands of the tiny one-eighth-by-one-quarter-inch beads in a wampum belt, and some fine examples can be seen in the New York State Museum. Wampum continued to be used as money until the mid-eighteenth century, when machine-produced wampum made it too plentiful to permit it to keep its value.

Shaping the Clam in Pastry

In the world of Italian pastry we discover "sfogliatelle," a word denoting folding. This pastry is shaped by layers and layers of very thin dough folded into the form of a clam, then filled with wonderful custards. I'm told by Ernie Marzullo, whose family runs the well-known Marzullo's Pastry Shop in New Haven, that the ability to fashion "sfogliatelle" is *the* critical test for someone to be accepted officially as an Italian pastry maker. Given where I rate clams, this highest hurdle seems very appropriate.

Swimming Habits of Scallops

Of all the bivalves that can swim as well as burrow with their foot, the scallop spends the most time swimming. You may have wondered why you see scallops sometimes swimming along and at other times simply lying on the bottom. A recent study of the swimming habits of bay scallops has shed new light on them. Many factors come into play, including the weight the scallop's topside shell acquires from the shell-encrusting organisms, the type of bottom (e.g., sand or grass), the interactions or potential interactions with predators, and the time intervals between one swim and the next, a kind of "fatigue factor," as it were. Writing in the *Journal of Experimental Marine Biology and Ecology*, (1985, vol. 88, pp. 227–242), M. A. Winter and P. V. Hamilton offer a very good description of the swimming of bay scallops: "Swimming begins with the rapid and repeated closure of the valves [known as] 'clapping.' When the valves are drawn together by the single adductor muscle, water is forced out of the mantle cavity and the scallop is propelled into the water column. Clapping continues for the remainder of the active swim. After a scallop ceases clapping, it glides back to the substratum passively, following a series of lateral slips (i.e., like a coin dropping through water)."

Scallops are known to swim to better environments, which explains why they disappear when the eelgrass is poor. They like to "recess" or rest in a small depression on the bottom. The authors discovered that scallops clearly travel to get into the grasses and away from the open sandy bottoms. In the grasses they find not only food, but greater protection. The combination of good eating and camouflage is well worth the travel, particularly because "bay scallops normally rest with their darkly pigmented left valve facing upward," so its shell is best camouflaged in a grass bed.

Veligers and Gastropods

I would like to get back to the beginning form of clams, namely the tiny pear-shaped veliger, or free-swimming larva from which the clams grow into the shelled creatures we eat, and to their existence in the Gastropoda class. I happily discovered a wonderfully apt poem whose punch line should be remembered by all who like to think about the curious anatomy of clams and other mollusks.

From the 1860s through World War I a large number of natural history journals were published in England, with the result that more and more species, including fossilized species, of mollusks were identified. This activity produced, along the way, the first publication of *The Journal of Conchology* in 1874, the formation of the Conchological Society of Great Britain and Ireland in 1876, and eventually, to the accumulation of a great shell collection at Leeds University. There, Professor Walter Garstang (1868–1949), who assumed the chair of zoology in 1907, probably was instrumental in having the surviving founders of the Society get honorary degrees. Garstang is the author of a book entitled (and this is surely a trivia question) *Larval Forms and Other Zoological Verses,* which was published by Blackwells of Oxford in 1951, poems with scientifically correct information designed to make it easier for students to remember the facts.

In 1928, Professor Garstang wrote one of his best, explaining how certain mollusks, in this case gastropods, develop from the larval stage until they end up with a foot sticking out from the bottom of their shells. Here is the poem, as reprinted in an article by A. Norris entitled "An Historical Record of Yorkshire Mollusca" in *Journal of Conchology,* vol. 32, part 1, April, 1985.

The Ballad of the Veliger, or
How the Gastropod Got Its Twist

The Veliger's a lively tar, the liveliest afloat,
A whirling wheel on either side propels his little boat;
But when the danger signal warns his bustling submarine,
He stops the engine, shuts the port, and drops below unseen.

He's witnessed several changes in pelagic motor-craft;
The first he sailed was just a tub, with a tiny cabin aft.
An archi-mollusk fashioned it, according to his kind,
He's always stowed his gills and things in a mantle-sac behind.

Young Archi-mollusk went to sea with nothing but a velum—
A sort of autocycling hoop, instead of pram—to wheel 'em;
And, spinning round, they one by one acquired parental features,
A shell above, a foot below—the queerest little creatues.

Clams Come Ashore

Every so often enormous numbers of clams are washed up on beaches, and there are no definitive explanations for the phenomenon. One of the greatest shore-comings of clams took place in the great eruption of 1909 when there was a "plague" of clams at Newport, Rhode Island. Some 2000 tons of clams were removed from the beach. At Sandy Hook, on March 5, 1979, over 180 million surf clams were washed ashore. These massive "strandings" of clams remain subjects of scientific inquiry. Evidently changes in tidal motions and salinity are involved, but they only partly explain it: the enormity of these clam shore invasions is such that more research is needed.

Look Out for a Forked-tail Horseshoe Crab

The horseshoe crab, frequently encountered when clamming, is not a crab but in fact a member of the phylum Arthropoda. The horseshoe crab is very, very old, going back as a species at least two hundred million years to the Triassic Period (the beginning of the Age of Dinosaurs), and even farther, probably 350 to 400 million years, to their earlier ancestors. Recently two marine scientists, Cynthia Johnson and Peter Kube, came upon a horseshoe crab on the beach in Southampton, Long Island, that had a tail with a fork or second tail. They reviewed the literature and found only six other references to horseshoe crabs with forked tails. The researchers suspect that the second tail began to grow when the first was injured, and that it was not an example of genetic mutation. However, how can we be sure? And how can we be certain that there did not once exist horseshoe crabs with forked tails for righting themselves and maneuvering? This is the kind of curiosity that anyone clamming should ponder, and it suggests that we should always be on the lookout for slight variations in creatures we encounter when clamming, including clams themselves. There are many unknowns in the ocean.

What About Heart Rate?

Because we live in an age of pulse-taking, when people are apt to tell you what their pulse is even before you might ask, I can't help being curious about the data on bivalves. I have to confess I am relying on published data, as I have neither done EKG's nor held a stethoscope to the clam. Here are the beats per minute of some of our favorites: steamer—5–14 range (you can bet it's at 14 when you grab it); mussel—15–25; oyster—25–30; clam (pisidium sp)—60–75; scallop—22–50. Just for the record, the octopus pulse rate ranges from 12 to 59, and the whelk, on the other hand, only vacillates in the 5 to 8 category! Finally, the cockroach pulse ranges from 60 to 90, while the lobster's runs from 50 to 100, probably depending on how athletic a schedule it has.

Izaak Walton and "The Compleat Angler"

Given this book's heritage, it seems appropriate to say a few words about Izaak Walton and his immortal classic, *The Compleat Angler*. Published in 1653, when he was sixty and without his name on it, this world-famous "pastoral" book devoted to the joys and strategies of fishing was meticulously reworked by Walton, whose fifth and final personal edition came out in 1676 with the new title, *The Universal Angler*, containing also a discourse on fly-fishing by his friend Charles Cotton and the 1662 book, *The Experienced Angler*, by Robert Venable. Walton's classic went through three hundred more editions. Walton, who lived to be ninety, was mostly self-taught and the son of an alehouse keeper.

Toxic Metals in the Sea

There has been much debate among both research scientists and environmentalists regarding the extent to which our seafood is dangerously contaminated by "toxic" metals in the sea. One of the most recent analyses of this controversy, "The Non-Toxicity of Metals to Animals in the Sea," by Willard Bascom, concludes convincingly that sea creatures generally have the ability sufficiently to "detoxify metals at the cellular level by means of a protein named metal-lothionein." For over ten years Bascom has overseen experiments involving thousands of sea creatures in highly contaminated areas—and "in all that work we have seen no recognizable evidence of damage to sea organisms by metals."

Metals in open coastal waters are simply not that much to worry about (reported in *Shore and Beach*, vol. 50, no. 2, April 1982).

Strange Bedfellows? Clams and Toadfish

In a recent research project it was determined that the toadfish *Opsanus tau* could be used successfully to control predation on the hard-shelled clam, *Mercenaria mercenaria*. Hard clams enclosed in beds with toadfish did much better than clams left to their own defenses. The point is that toadfish successfully eliminate the crabs that commonly prey upon clams, particularly where they are found in abundance. This is a perfect example of the possibilities for biological control situations, using one kind of animal to strengthen the cultivation of another. By placing nets over clam beds and keeping toadfish in the area, clams will be better grown and harvested (as reported in M. C. Gibbons and M. Castagna, "Biological Control of Predation by Crabs in Bottom Cultures of Hard Clams Using a Combination of Crushed Stone Aggregate, Toadfish, and Cages," *Aquaculture*, vol. 47, nos. 2/3, July 1985).

Why Don't Americans Eat the Entire Scallop?

Out of curiosity I asked Captain Frank Beckwith why he thought people in this country don't eat the whole scallop, while many other peoples do. He was not certain, but he had fun speculating. Back in the old days of scalloping the shells were stacked in enormous piles where the remains were eaten by cats. Most of

the cats he and others remember seeing on the scallop shell piles seemed to have their ears falling off, so Frank suggests people might have believed the same thing would happen to them if they ate more than the traditional white center muscle!

Indians and Clams

Native American Indians enjoyed clambakes—also a subject of Winslow Homer woodcuts in 1873—long before they demonstrated them to the white men settling the North American continent. The Indians knew how to roast in the sand and were experts as well at preparing food for long travels, sometimes a thousand miles, for example, out of Puget Sound, their canoes loaded with fish, seaweed, roots, dried berries, and clams. They also found many uses for clam shells beyond wampum. In both eating and using clams, the Indians were simply carrying forward ancient customs from the days of early man. The Pygmies of Gabon, for many centuries, used the shell of a large sand snail for cutting out the hearts of small animals being sacrificed in rituals and for circumcising babies.

Filling Tubs with Clams and Moving Up to ''Bumboating''

Captain Frank Beckwith remembers well what it was like to clam in the early 1930s. Once he came upon a good-sized bed of littlenecks, which he worked very hard to dig up over a period of three days. He filled eighteen "tubs" (butter tubs, in which clams were marketed and which held about three pecks of clams). As was the way, someone came to Shelter Island and picked up the filled tubs, then ferried them to Greenport, where they were loaded onto trucks and taken to New York City. For his work, Frank received $4.18.

Not too much later, Frank took the recommendation of a friend and began his "bumboating" work, meaning that he would go out to all the yachts in the harbor, ask them what they wanted (ice, eggs, milk, and so forth), get the order, then deliver it the next morning. Since the alternative was for the yachtsmen to go either to Greenport or to Sag Harbor to get their own ice and supplies, they were glad for the service. Before long, Frank had given up clamming and was making ten dollars a day. And in those days a 300-pound block of ice sold for a dollar.

Sexual Maturity

Trivial as it should be, bivalves reach sexual maturity at different rates, and it is absolutely nonessential to know the following differences regarding who gets to first base, as it were, first. The bay scallop leads the pack, reaching sexual maturity in one year. The hard-shelled clam, the soft-shelled clam, and the mussel all take one to two years. For the razor clam *Siliqua patula* of the eastern Pacific it's a 2–4.2-year period, while the Pismo clam of the Pacific area takes a whopping five years.

Shell Cameos

Carving cameos from shells has been practised for at least four hundred years, and many different shells of different color and lustre have been used. Most cameo shells were made as decorative pieces, not to be worn. The master cameo carver, Francesco Bruno, of Trapani, Sicily, produced a very famous shell cameo in 1902. Displayed in connection with the celebration of the centenary of Victor Hugo, the cameo contained lines from Hugo's classic, *Les Miserables*. In the Renaissance, mussels were used for cameo shell art, but today the main shells are the Horned Helmet, Red Helmet, Queen Conch, and King Helmet. Their high lustre rivals that of pearls. Most cameos today are carved in Naples.

Pearls Then and Now

Pearls have long been revered, and references to their high value appear in the Bible, the Talmud, and the Koran. An excellent *National Geographic* article by Fred Ward (August 1985) provides a well-illustrated and comprehensive summary of the pearl throughout the ages. Ward notes that the pearl was, on the one hand, one of the very first gems to adorn mankind, while, on the other, Australian aborigines hated biting into pearls when eating oysters; they considered them worthless (though their children played with them as marbles). Ward further notes, "Before 3500 B.C., when American Indians and European tribesmen huddled in caves, civilized Mideast and Asian societies treasured pearls as supremely valuable possessions, rhapsodizing over them as symbols of purity, chastity, and feminine charms. Later, from the financial and marketing center in Bombay, the jewels found their way into royal collections throughout India, Persia, Egypt, and beyond."

Today pearls are grown commercially in many places both abroad and at home, but perhaps most successfully in the large South Sea oysters that reach a foot in diameter and produce pearls measuring up to 20 millimeters. "Master of the Pearl," an account of the life and accomplishments of Kokichi Mikimoto, appears in *Oceans* (no. 3, 1984) and is highly recommended. Two things are certain: Despite their easier availability and their commercially cultivated status, pearls will continue to hold a fascination for man, and you can still come across one by surprise when opening either oysters or mussels.

Final Note to the Reader

There are undoubtedly many interesting but trivial additions one could make to this chapter, and I would be interested seriously in receiving any suggestions from readers that I promise to consider for publication in future editions. Just drop me a line with suggestions, or with any other points about clams and clamming, care of Nick Lyons Books, 31 West 21st Street, New York, NY 10010. As I mentioned at the outset, I enjoy learning all I can and keep deepening my enjoyment of clamming by knowing more about them.

Appendix:
Clamming Regulations

          As noted in chapter 1, it is very important to know the rules and regulations that govern gathering clams and other shellfish in different coastal localities. It is always a good idea to check with the nearest community town hall, if there is one, and learn about permit requirements, quota and legal-size rules, and any other guidelines or restrictions. Since every community is governed a bit differently, the best way to check on what you want to do and where you want to do it is to be in touch by letter or phone with the appropriate state regulatory agency. Some states have statutes that govern size (e.g., Connecticut) whereas *towns* set other laws. Many states have different regulations. In New Hampshire you need to be a resident of the state. In Rhode Island you not only don't have to be a resident, you don't need any kind of permit. In Massachusetts town rules govern. In Georgia you can go freshwater clamming and look for pearls in larger mussels. In Virginia an individual can take 250 clams, while in some states it's by the peck or bushel. In Alabama there are no regulations, but no dredges are allowed. What follows is the most accurate information available as we go to press. It covers all the coastal states of this country in alphabetical order.

ALABAMA
Department of Conservation and
  Natural Resources
Division of Marine Resources
P.O. Box 189
Dauphin Island, AL 36528
Phone: 205-861-2882

ALASKA
Department of Fish and Game
P.O. Box 3-2000
Juneau, AK 99802
*Phone: 907-465-4100 (Sport Fish
  Div. 907-465-4180)*

CALIFORNIA
Department of Fish and Game
Division of Marine Resources
1416 Ninth Street
Sacramento, CA 95814
Phone: 916-324-9676

CONNECTICUT
Department of Aquaculture
Rogers Avenue
Milford, CT 06460-6499
Phone: 203-874-0696
Note: Recreational clamming in
Connecticut is administered by
the towns, so they recommend
contacting the town clerk; state
statutes pertain to size. The state
department of health services
publishes a booklet describing
areas certified for harvesting.
Contact Malcolm Shute, Director, Connecticut State Department of Health Services, Environmental Health Section,
150 Washington Street, Hart-
ford, CT 06106. Phone:
203-566-1258.
Director, Connecticut State
Fisheries Bureau, *phone:*
203-566-2287

DELAWARE
Mrs. Freeman
Department of Natural
  Resources and Environmental
  Control
Division of Fish and Wildlife
  (Attention: Fisheries section)
P.O. Box 1401
Dover, DE 19903
Phone: 302-736-3441

FLORIDA
Shellfish Administration
Department of Natural
  Resources
Room 813
3900 Commonwealth Blvd.
Tallahassee, FL 32303
Phone: 904-488-6058
Alternately: Captain Louis Shelfer,
  phone: 904-488-9284

GEORGIA
Department of Natural
  Resources
Law Enforcement
Coastal Resources Division
1200 Glynn Avenue
Brunswick, GA 31523
Phone: 912-264-7237

LOUISIANA
(governing oysters, not clams)
Department of Wildlife and
  Fisheries
P.O. Box 15570
Baton Rouge, LA 70895
Phone: 504-342-9280

MAINE
Maine Department of Marine
  Resources
State House
Station 21
Augusta, ME 04333
Phone: 207-289-2291

MARYLAND
Department of Natural
  Resources
Tawes State Office Building
Tidewater Administration
Annapolis, MD 21401
Phone: 301-269-2926

MASSACHUSETTS
Division of Marine Fisheries
Leverett Saltonstall Building
Government Center
100 Cambridge Street
Boston, MA 02202
Phone: Director of Sport Fisheries,
  617-727-3193

MISSISSIPPI
Bureau of Marine Fisheries
P.O. Drawer 959
Long Beach, MS 39560
Phone: 601-864-4602

NEW HAMPSHIRE
New Hampshire Fish and Game
34 Bridge Street
Concord, NH 03301
Attention: Chief, Inland and
  Marine Fisheries
Phone: 603-271-3421

NEW JERSEY
Department of Environmental
  Protection
Bureau of Shellfisheries
CN 400
Trenton, NJ 08625
Phone: 609-292-1055

NEW YORK
NYS Department of
  Environmental Conservation
Bureau of Shellfisheries
Building 40, SUNY
Stony Brook, NY 11794
Phone: 516-751-7900

Appendix

NORTH CAROLINA
North Carolina Co-operative
    Fisheries Research Unit
North Carolina State
    University, Box 7617
Raleigh, North Carolina
    27695-7617
Attention: Dr. Mel Huish or Dr.
    Kirby
Phone: 919-737-2631
or:
Division of Marine Fisheries
P.O. Box 769
Moorehead City, NC 28557
*Phone: 919-737-2741 (Extension
    Fisheries Specialist)*

OREGON
Department of Fish and Wildlife
Marine Science Drive Building 3
Newport, OR 97365
Phone: 503-867-4741
*Also: Asst. Director of Fisheries:
    503-229-5440*

RHODE ISLAND
Department of Environmental
    Management
Division of Fish and Wildlife
Washington County
    Government Center
Tower Hill Road
Wakefield, RI 02879
Phone: 401-789-3094

SOUTH CAROLINA
South Carolina Department of
    Wildlife and Marine
    Resources
P.O. Box 167
Columbia, SC 29202
Phone: 795-803-6350

TEXAS
Texas Parks and Wildlife
    Department
Coastal Fisheries Division
4200 Smith School Road
Austin, TX 78744
Phone: 512-479-4857

VIRGINIA
Virginia Marine Resources
    Comm.
Law Enforcement Division
P.O. Box 756
2401 West Avenue
Newport News, VA 23607
Phone: 804-247-2200

WASHINGTON
Department of Fisheries
115 General Administration
    Building
Olympia, WA 98504
Phone: 206-753-6749
*Also, Asst. Director, Shellfish,
    206-753-6749*

Index